FOURTH HURDLE
CONSULTING LIMITED

2 Fisher Street, Holborn,
London WC1R 4QA.
Tel: +44 (0)20 7440 4060

HEALTH STATUS MEAS
A PERSPECTIVE ON CHANGE

ECONOMIC ISSUES IN HEALTH CARE

General editors

Professor Gavin Mooney
Department of Community Medicine
Westmead Hospital
Westmead, NSW 2145
Australia

Dr Alistair McGuire
Deparment of Economics
City University
Nottingham Square
London EC1V 0HB

The Challenges of Medical Practice Variations
Edited by Tavs Folmer Andersen and Gavin Mooney (1990)

Competition in Health Care: Reforming the NHS
Edited by A.J. Culyer, Alan Maynard and John Posnett (1990)

Strategies for Health Care Finance in Developing Countries
By Guy Carrin with Marc Vereecke (1992)

Private Exchange and Public Interest
By John Forbes (1992)

Just Managing – Power and Culture in the NHS
By Stephen Harrison, David J. Hunter and Gordon Marnoch (1992)

Economics of Health Care Financing: The Visible Hand
By Cam Donaldson and Karen Gerard (1992)

Rationing and Rationality in the National Health Service
Edited by Stephen J. Frankel and R.R. West (1993)

Health Status Measurement: A Perspective on Change
By Richard G. Brooks (1995)

HEALTH STATUS MEASUREMENT: A PERSPECTIVE ON CHANGE

Richard G. Brooks

Department of Economics
University of Strathclyde

© Richard G. Brooks 1995

All rights reserved. No reproduction, copy or transmission of this publication may be made without written permission.

No paragraph of this publication may be reproduced, copied or transmitted save with written permission or in accordance with the provisions of the Copyright, Designs and Patents Act 1988, or under the terms of any licence permitting limited copying issued by the Copyright Licensing Agency, 90 Tottenham Court Road, London W1P 9HE.

Any person who does any unauthorised act in relation to this publication may be liable to criminal prosecution and civil claims for damages.

First published 1995 by
MACMILLAN PRESS LTD
Houndmills, Basingstoke, Hampshire RG21 2XS
and London
Companies and representatives
throughout the world

ISBN 0–333–52719–4 hardcover
ISBN 0–333–52720–8 paperback

A catalogue record for this book is available from the British Library.

10	9	8	7	6	5	4	3	2	1
04	03	02	01	00	99	98	97	96	95

Printed in Great Britain by
Antony Rowe Ltd
Chippenham, Wiltshire

Series Standing Order (Economic Issues in Health Care)

If you would like to receive future titles in this series as they are published, you can make use of our standing order facility. To place a standing order please contact your bookseller or, in case of difficulty, write to us at the address below with your name and address and the name of the series. Please state with which title you wish to begin your standing order. (If you live outside the UK we may not have the rights for your area, in which case we will forward your order to the publisher concerned.)

Standing Order Service, Macmillan Distribution Ltd,
Houndmills, Basingstoke, Hampshire, RG21 2XS, England

In memory of my mother

Contents

List of Figures	viii
List of Tables	ix
Acknowledgements	x
Preface	xi
List of Abbreviations and Acronyms	xii
1 The Upsurge of Interest in Health Status Measurement	1
2 An Outline of the Development of Health Status Measures	15
3 Methodology	45
4 Quality as an Issue	57
5 The Measurement Process	71
6 Implications for Decision-Making	90
7 Trends and Issues	102
Concluding Remarks	122
References	125
Index	137

Figures

2.1	Functional status questionnaire	22
2.2	Functional status report: sample	23
2.3	AIMS questionnaire	39
3.1	Functional assessments: guidelines for evaluation	50
4.1	An analytic strategy for research on the quality of mental health services	59
5.1	Euroqol: own health state measure	75
5.2	Standard gamble for a chronic health state preferred to death	77
5.3	Time trade-off for a chronic health state preferred to death	80
5.4	Quality-adjusted life-years added by treatment	83
7.1	A conceptual scheme for valuation in health	116

Tables

1.1	Types of economic evaluation	3
2.1	Functional assessment instruments	20
2.2	Functional assessment measures: some examples of coverage	20
2.3	The Bush index: function levels and associated levels of well-being	25
2.4	The Bush index: symptom-problem complexes	29
2.5	Rosser's classification of illness states	31
2.6	Rosser's valuation matrix for 70 respondents	31
2.7	Generic measures: aggregate	33
2.8	Health profiles: an outline	34
2.9	Stages in development of two models for measuring quality of life	36
2.10	Disease specific measures	37
2.11	Sample items from the Mental Health Inventory (MHI)	42
2.12	Mental instruments	42
4.1	Rheumatology standards	62
5.1	Euroqol: results of three pilot studies	88
7.1	Frequency of usage of measurement instruments	104
7.2	Quality adjusted life-year (QALY) of competing therapies: some tentative estimates	113

Acknowledgements

I would like to thank the editors of the series, Alistair McGuire and Gavin Mooney, for their substantial contributions to the shape and contents of the book. Gavin originally suggested (over liquid refreshment in Nyhavn, Copenhagen) that I write the book, and then provided valuable comments as the book took shape. Ali was most helpful in reviewing and commenting upon an entire draft of the book.

I am very grateful to the personnel at the Swedish Institute for Health Economics for making me welcome over a number of years at their excellent facilities in Lund: a lot of the background work for the book was undertaken there. Björn Lindgren, the former director of the Institute, has my special thanks for stimulating my interest in health status measurement in the first place and then for giving me every encouragement to keep up this interest.

I would like to thank three of my former students at the Department of Economics, University of Strathclyde, for their assistance: Angela Boland, Clare Reid and Lesley Corrigan. Lesley was especially helpful during the final stages of preparation of the manuscript, including the reference list and the index. I would like also to acknowledge the financial assistance provided by the *Journal of Economic Studies* Fund at the University of Strathclyde.

All sins of omission and commission are, of course, my responsibility.

Permission to include the following material is gratefully acknowledged:

Figures 2.1 and 2.2: Alan Jette and the *Journal of General Internal Medicine*.
Figure 2.3: J.B. Lippincott Company.
Figure 3.1 and Table 4.1: Clare Bombardier and the *Journal of Rheumatology*.
Figure 4.1: Elizabeth McGlynn and *Inquiry*.
Figure 5.3: George Torrance and Elsevier Science Publications.
Figure 5.4: Mike Drummond.
Tables 2.3 and 2.4: Reprinted with permission from the Hospital Research and Educational Trust.
Tables 2.5 and 2.6: Claire Gudex and Paul Kind.
Table 2.9: Gordon Guyatt.
Table 2.11: John Ware.
Table 7.2: Alan Maynard.

Preface

This book is about the development of outcome measures in health, with particular emphasis on health status and health-related quality of life measurement. It is explicitly concerned to place this development within the changing context of the health world, not least its relevance to the changing requirements of health care decision-making at all levels.

Starting with an economic framework which encompasses the requirement to match costs with outcomes, the question is addressed: why has there been such an upsurge of interest in health status measurement in handling outcomes? The present situation is placed into its historical context by showing how health status measures have developed from the early attempts at functional assessment in the 1940s and 1950s. A variety of health status and health-related quality-of-life measures are illustrated and discussed. The methodological requirements for 'sound' health status measurement are outlined, and the measurement process itself — commonly referred to as 'scaling' — is reviewed. Any reading of the burgeoning literature in this field will provide ample evidence of the pervasiveness of the attempts to define, conceptualise, and measure 'quality' as it pertains to the use of resources in the health sector and in the notion of (health-related) quality of life. Issues surrounding quality are thus given some attention. The final two chapters cover a wide range of issues surrounding health status measurement, its place in health services research, and its implications for decision-making.

RICHARD G. BROOKS

Abbreviations and Acronyms

ADL	Activities of daily living
AIMS	Arthritis Impact Measurement Scale
C	Celsius
CS	Category scaling
CBA	Cost-benefit analysis
CEA	Cost-effectiveness analysis
CR	Category rating
CUA	Cost-utility analysis
DOMPS	Diseases of medical progress
DUHP	Duke–UNC Health Profile
ESR	Erythrocyte sedimentation rate
F	Fahrenheit
FDA	Food and Drug Administration
FLP	Functional Limitations Profile
FSI	Functional Status Index
FSQ	Functional Status Questionnaire
GHQ	General Health Questionnaire
HAQ	Health Assessment Questionnaire
HCFA	Health Care and Financing Administration
HYE	Healthy year equivalent
IADL	Instrumental activities of daily living
IHQL	Index of Health-Related Quality of Life
JCAH	Joint Commission on Accreditation of Hospitals
ME	Magnitude estimation
MHAQ	Modified Health Assessment Questionnaire
MHI	Mental Health Inventory
NHP	Nottingham Health Profile
QA	Quality assurance
QALY	Quality adjusted life-year
QWB	Quality of well-being
RAWP	Resource Allocation Working Party
RCT	Randomised control trial
RS	Rating scale

SAVE	Saved young life equivalent
SG	Standard gamble
SIP	Sickness Impact Profile
TA	Technology assessment
TTO	Time trade-off
UK	United Kingdom
US(A)	United States of America
VAS	Visual analogue scale
WHO	World Health Organisation

CHAPTER 1

The Upsurge of Interest in Health Status Measurement

Why has there been such an upsurge of interest in studying and measuring health status and health-related quality of life in recent years? This book addresses this question and explores the changing issues surrounding the evaluation of resource use in health. It might be asked at the outset why this question is worth answering. After all, medical personnel deal with health status throughout their working lives. Saving people's lives, making people feel better: what more justification is required for health intervention, for the services of doctors and nurses, the popping of pills, the strapping of injured limbs, the words of comfort, the plastercasts? Why go any further in explaining the 'need' for medical and other interventions which may fundamentally affect health and well-being: if medical care is needed then surely we would expect resources to be devoted to its supply?

But then, what is 'health', what is 'health status'? What is 'need' in this context? Are the medical and allied health professions agreed on how resources might or should be used for health interventions? Are all agreed on the appropriate procedures for use in handling and treating disease and disability? Should medical practitioners be constrained in their actions? Are the outcomes of health sector resource use clear and obvious? Further, how have attitudes to all these issues, and how have customs and practices, changed over time?

These are not (meant to be) rhetorical questions. Nobody reading the medical and related literature or who is involved in any way with health and the health sector could believe that there are clearcut answers to the fundamental issues of the definition of health and health status and medical (and other) needs, and attempting to give answers to the other questions posed involves significant study, investigation and deliberation.

One major reason for an economist to write this book is that economists continually seek to address the questions of choice that must be made in a world of scarcity. If we could do everything 'desirable' in health or education or defence or manufacturing or leisure we would presumably do just that. A world of abundant resources would not pose problems of choice. Hospitals, for example, could be full of all the latest technology to be used on demand on behalf of patients. A moment's thought indicates that this is a world unrecognisable to us. Choices must be made: we can always do nothing or do something. More specifically, we can continue allocating and using resources in the manner to which we have become accustomed, perhaps over long periods of time, or we can change, and change is of course the theme of the series of which this book is a part.

AN ECONOMIC FRAMEWORK

Let us introduce an economic framework to put health status and quality-of-life measurement into perspective. It should be pointed out at the outset that this is only one possible frame of reference, but it is clearly an appropriate one in the context of this series of books. The economic evaluation in the taxonomy presented could in principle be used for any programme which influences or could influence health status: the framework need not be confined to medical care decisions or even to health sector decisions as such. It can encompass prevention, promotion, community work or any other use of resources with health and health-related welfare as the intended goals.

Essentially the aim of all economic evaluation in health is to link the inputs going into a project or procedure with the outputs resulting from the use of these inputs. It is not sufficient for *evaluation* to focus on one side of the 'account' (say the costs of the inputs) to the exclusion of the other side: there must be the link, preferably made explicit and not just left implicit. We shall eschew the use of the term 'outputs' in this book, redolent as it is of physical images, such as cars or washing machines. Instead we will refer to 'outcomes', a suitably neutral word, it is hoped, when dealing with human beings. Although whether our very human feelings and foibles can be captured by concentrating on the outcomes of health interventions is an issue to which we will return more than once during the course of the book!

The taxonomy is: cost analysis, cost minimisation analysis, cost-effectiveness analysis (CEA), cost-utility analysis (CUA), and cost-benefit analysis (CBA). The nature of these methods of evaluation is outlined in Table 1.1. Note that all of these techniques include costs. Since we are concerned with economic evaluation, an assessment of the alternatives in resource use is required. Explanations of the measurement of costs focus strongly on the notion of *opportunity cost*. The opportunity cost of an action is the value of the next best alternative use of the resource or resources used in that action: the opportunity costs to the author in writing this book certainly include the value of some of his leisure time, for example! Resources committed to one health programme have their costs in terms of the forgone alternatives, often the value of other health interventions. Much effort is expended in economic evaluation in identifying and measuring the opportunity costs of alternative activities.

If *social* evaluation is contemplated then it is necessary to include the word 'social' before each of these techniques – if it is society's interests we

Table 1.1 Types of economic evaluation

Type of evaluation	Cost measurement	Outcome measurement	Outcome valuation
Cost-minimisation	Pounds (£)	Assumed equivalent	No valuation
Cost-effectiveness	Pounds (£)	Outcome common to alternatives being evaluated, but achieved to different degrees	Common units e.g. number of lives saved, days of disability avoided
Cost-benefit	Pounds (£)	Any effects produced by the alternatives	Pounds (£)
Cost-utility	Pounds (£)	Single or multiple effects, common or unique to the alternatives and achieved to differing degrees	QALYs, well years, other utility measures

Source: Adapted from Drummond *et al.*, 1987.

have at heart, the attempt should be made to evaluate costs and outcomes within the social framework. To give a medical care example: a health board considering building a new clinic, say, will be concerned to assess the capital and running costs of the clinic and will judge whether its budget in terms of the potential financial outlays can be expected to meet these costs. But for certain decisions patient costs may be a crucial factor, as is the case where hospital provision is changed so that it is proposed that existing institutions close and new ones be opened, sometimes quite far apart geographically. This may well impose significant changes in the pattern of travel costs. A social appraisal ought to take account of such changes and not simply the impact of the project on the health board's budget. Similarly, for social outcome evaluation a wider viewpoint should be taken than that of the individuals affected by the resource allocation decision. Strictly speaking it does not matter whether such a project be privately or publicly financed: a social appraisal would take this wider viewpoint. Whether health projects should be publicly financed or not will not be considered here.

Cost Analysis

If the effectiveness of different methods of achieving an outcome can be assumed to be exactly the same then the relative costs of these methods can be compared. This is a rather limited approach but will suffice for what might be viewed as 'technical' decisions, such as different ways of supply-

Cost Minimisation Analysis

Here the effectiveness of, say, alternative therapies is not known initially, but can be shown to be equivalent by a controlled clinical trial. Another example would be comparing the cost of day surgery with surgery involving an inpatient stay where the same operation is performed and the same outcome results. In these sorts of cases the allocation decision would turn on the costs involved and the alternative minimising the cost would be appropriate.

Cost-Effectiveness Analysis (CEA)

Suppose, though, clinical effects were to differ? So that, for example, different projects or programmes produced different numbers of life-years gained. Then cost-effectiveness approaches are required: maximise life-years gained for given resources (costs) or minimise costs for a given goal, e.g. a particular number of life-years saved – the latter version being little different from cost minimisation analysis as outlined above.

This approach has been used in numerous evaluation studies. A recent bibliography (Backhouse *et al.*, 1992) showed CEA to be the largest single category of economic evaluation at 580 references, 30.7 per cent of the total compiled.

It is evident that as we move through these approaches we encounter more 'sophistication' on the outcome side, but there is little yet in the way of valuation, unless 'life-years', say, are used as a numeraire in cost-effectiveness studies: but this constitutes a very limited form of valuation.

Cost-Utility Analysis (CUA)

The relatively restrictive nature of these versions of CEA becomes clear as soon as we ask: 'what about the *quality* of life?' This is a crucial question and this book considers in some detail the issues surrounding the answers. The trade-off between length of life and quality of life can be a key issue in health intervention, a classic example being the choice between chemotherapy and surgical treatment in cancer treatment. At issue is whether cancer sufferers would prefer shorter 'higher quality' life to longer 'lower quality' life, and alternative treatment scenarios can produce such trade-offs. The explicit attention paid to quality adjustment and to the nature of health status led to the use of the term cost-utility analysis (CUA) to cover such evaluation. It should be stressed that the term 'utility' has an all-embracing status in principle, if not necessarily in practice for some of the specific health status measures that have been devised. The concept of utility is commonly used in economics and philosophy, amongst other disciplines, to cover *inter alia*: happiness, satisfaction, well-being, and welfare. The most common outcome measure employed in cost-utility analysis has been the quality-adjusted lifeyear (QALY): Chapters 5 and 7 deal in some detail with this concept and its ramifications. It should be evident that within our economic framework CUA could be taken to represent an extension or broadening-out of CEA.

Although only 3 per cent of the evaluation papers listed in the recent major survey were of the CUA type (Backhouse *et al.*, 1992) the figures show that as many of these studies were carried out in the first eighteen months of the 1990s as in the whole of the 1980s, a trend of distinct relevance for the present book.

Cost-Benefit Analysis (CBA)

Another line to pursue would be monetary evaluation on the outcome side, as well as on the input or cost side, which leads on to CBA. In principle every aspect of a health project or programme could be valued using a monetary 'unit of account' such as the pound, deutschmark or dollar. It is important to stress that this does not necessarily mean that money changes hands, simply that a monetary unit is being used for evaluation purposes. If the unit of account was the cigarette (apparently the case in prisoner-of-war camps in the Second World War, if elementary economics textbooks are to be believed) or money made of coal (a medium of exchange used in Germany during the hyperinflation of the 1920s) then we would be comparing costs with outcomes in numbers of cigarettes or in coal units in order to make a judgement concerning whether the value of the outcomes exceeded the value of the resources used.

CBA holds out the promise of a very broad evaluative framework, because with a unit of account available with which to measure health interventions then alternative actions can be compared quite readily, and indeed 'one-off' propositions can be judged: if a surplus of benefits over costs is predicted from a project then it is likely to be worth undertaking because social welfare would be increased by so doing. Note again that it is the *social* evaluation of health interventions that is being considered.

Many cost-benefit studies have been conducted across a wide range of health interventions, with 10 per cent of evaluation studies using this approach (Backhouse *et al.*, 1992).

The emphasis on monetary evaluation, however, can make CBA appear restrictive or, for some analysts, unethical. Nevertheless, whilst earlier enthusiasm for the CBA approach has perhaps subsided somewhat, a considerable volume of work is being undertaken on such matters as the valuation of life, or perhaps more accurately the valuation of risks to life and livelihood, and on the question of how to measure people's willingness to pay in the context of health and health-related services. In recent years the willingness-to-pay approach has been treated or classified as a form of 'scaling' or valuation in health status measurement, so further reference is made to this approach in Chapter 5.

Although something of a revival of interest in the cost-benefit approach can be discerned lately, and although CEA retains its popularity, the changing emphasis in economic appraisal in recent years has been quite strongly towards CUA. One reason for this may be the argument that the efforts to find utility evaluations by all sorts of methods are even more fundamental and comprehensive in scope precisely because the emphasis is on determining the meaning of utility and quality of life in the health context and, more importantly for evaluation, measuring these entities. Utility could be viewed as a unifying concept in the sense that all stages of a medical 'event' can be conceived of as yielding utility or its downside counterpart, disutility: treatment can of course be unpleasant. If it is possible to measure utility and disutility in some agreed manner then we would be able to evaluate and compare health interventions using a common measurement framework. It should again be stressed that the notion of utility is not a specifically economic concept, having had a long history in moral philosophy.

Another reason could be relief amongst economists at the chance to move away from a method that appears to 'price' everything connected with a health intervention, thus incurring opprobrium for those willing to advocate CBA. Be that as it may, the £ or $ sign will not go away and the concept of opportunity cost remains fully entrenched in economic evaluation.

It is evident, then, from this discussion that our economic framework requires appropriate outcome measures for evaluation purposes. The framework presented is by no means, however, a complete characterisation of all the necessary facets of evaluation. Some would argue that these economic techniques are notable for their emphasis on the 'efficient' use of resources, to the possible exclusion of, or at least the downplaying of, the distributional or equity issue of who gets what. This is not the place to report on the debate as to whether or not equity can or should be formally incorporated into the techniques outlined, but when concepts such as 'efficiency' are considered there may well be 'trade-offs' to contemplate. Some action which scores well on efficiency grounds may turn out to be highly inequitable, for example.

There is now a substantial body of work accomplished by a variety of disciplines on health care inequities or inequalities. Meanwhile quite formal criteria have been used in Britain to reallocate health sector resources, through the Resource Allocation Working Party (RAWP) procedure in England and

Wales, for example (Department of Health and Social Security, 1976). In principle it should be possible to incorporate health status measurement into such criteria. If at times health status measurement is viewed as controversial, then the criteria for the judgement of equity in this area are no less the subject of fierce debate!

In concluding this brief exposition of economic evaluation, and in anticipation of further commentary during the course of the book, it can be argued that there are essentially two views concerning quality of life, namely the descriptive and the evaluative. The descriptive approach constitutes an effort to encompass and measure all the elements constituting the quality of life. The evaluative approach is explicitly concerned with placing weights upon and *valuing* the relevant elements of health status and quality of life. It should be evident from the framework just described that economic appraisal is firmly placed within the evaluative domain. The question of relevance will be discussed in some detail throughout the book as we examine the principles and practice of measurement and valuation in the context of health status and quality of life.

THE DEFINITION OF HEALTH

Before outlining why health status measurement has expanded so rapidly in recent times it would be as well briefly to contemplate the meaning of 'health'. Hanslukwa (1985) provided a list of 20 views on the definition of health and the capacity to measure it. These include the famous World Health Organisation (WHO) definition of health as 'a state of complete physical, mental and social wellbeing and not merely the absence of infirmity' and views such as: 'health is not merely a state desirable in itself but is a means towards the fulfilment of strategic role obligations' (Ahmed *et al.* 1979). One look at these definitions indicates the potential complexity of answering the deceptively simple question: 'what is health?'. The enduring WHO definition is not unhelpful, however, as it points to the need to encompass mental and social 'wellbeing' as well as the physical. The development of health status and health-related quality-of-life measures undoubtedly represents one aspect of the striving towards the health entity for both analytical and policy purposes.

This minefield of conceptualisation and definition could perhaps be avoided by adopting an explicit utility framework as the 'unifying concept' noted above. Thus any changes in 'health' or 'ill-health' or 'disability' or 'function' can be captured by changes in a person's utility and, in principle, changes in the utility (and thus hopefully social welfare) of society as a whole. Unfortunately in skirting one minefield we enter another, that of defining and measuring both the utility of individuals and, even more controversial, societal utility or social welfare.

What is evident, whether we treat health and health status in some direct sense or within the utility framework, is that all these concepts are value-laden. Somebody or some group of people has to make judgements as to what constitutes an 'improvement' in health or an 'increase' in utility or welfare. Again, independent of the framework, much debate has taken place over whose values should be placed on health states, once these have been described. The actual description of health states is not without its controversies, but far more heat has been engendered over the 'whose values' issue. We shall return to these matters in subsequent chapters, especially Chapter 5, but suffice it to say that there are advocates for patients, for doctors and other health personnel, for the citizen, and for the politician!

THE RISING INTEREST IN HEALTH STATUS MEASUREMENT

If we contemplate change in medicine and health, why has there been such an explosion of interest in the issues of health status measurement in recent times? Evidence for this appears in the author's survey which contains over 700 references and even so cannot be regarded as fully comprehensive (Brooks, 1991). Another comprehensive bibliography is that of Spilker and associates (1990): this comprises 578 references.

Measurement of health status dates back to Babylonian times, but it is the development of health status measurement over the last 45 years and particularly the last 25 years which is the concern of this book. The pattern of development will be examined in Chapter 2, but first we can discuss several major areas where we can seek the reasons for this enhanced interest and concern: (*i*) quality of life, (*ii*) technological change, (*iii*) medical effectiveness, (*iv*) changes in health sector organisation and finance, (*v*) cultural developments. Each is treated in turn.

Quality of Life

For many years statistics have been routinely collected on population, births, mortality, and morbidity. Clearly, evaluation of health programmes and expenditures could be undertaken using the standard statistical indices. For matters of life and death, mortality data are crucial and may indeed be sufficient for the purpose at hand. Roberts (1990) lists a range of mortality measures: maternal, perinatal, hospital, and disease-specific mortality; population mortality rates; perioperative deaths, anaesthetic deaths; and suicide. Many health problems and their associated interventions are not, however, life-and-death matters. It is evident that in many countries chronic diseases have become increasingly prominent, thus leading the focus away from matters of mortality (which clearly remain dominant, however, for some diseases and conditions).

The notion that mortality should not necessarily be the focus of attention in assessing health outcomes is not a novel idea. In his textbook on health statistics Swaroop (1960) quotes Charles Dickens: 'It concerns a man more to know the risk of the fifty illnesses that may throw him on his back than the possible date of the one death that must come.'

Are morbidity indices, which attempt to measure sickness levels through data on illness and injuries, incapacitation, hospitalisation and so forth, sufficient for evaluation? No, many analysts would answer, citing the difficulty in assessing the degree of sickness in individuals and the problems of detecting the changes in the individual's 'sickness experience' or, more positively, health status over time. These are familiar themes. It is commonly asserted that there is an 'iceberg of sickness' so that much sickness or disease goes undetected or, at least, unrecorded in any formal way. Furthermore it is evident that the world is not divided neatly into the sick and the well: there is a continuum which may need investigation. Hence the need, it is asserted, for formal systematic health status and quality-of-life measurement.

Observe also, on a demographic note, that with life expectancy still continuing to rise in many countries, and certainly now much longer than in earlier times, we have the challenge of assessing the quality of life of people living longer and in so doing being prone to the conditions and diseases more likely to manifest themselves in old age.

Let us review the issues concerning the whys and wherefores of quality-of-life measurement within the cancer context, where important matters arise surrounding the inter-relationships between mortality and quality of life. We can do this with the help of McCartney and Larson (1987). They point out that without treatment cancer causes progressive deterioration of health, loss of function, and discomfort. Unfortunately, though, treatment may be associated with unpleasant side effects. These authors suggest that any measure of the effectiveness of treatment should include the quality of life so that individual patients' life priorities would become part of decisions about treatment. If cure is likely patients might be willing to tolerate these side effects because of the great benefit achieved, namely survival. If the treatment is palliative in nature some patients may still prefer treatment as in their judgement the benefits are worth the costs. On the other hand, and clearly relevant for our discussion, some patients may prefer shorter survival if this is associated with better quality of life. Another possibility is that where survival benefits are similar for two treatments then the predicted quality of life could influence the choice between the treatments.

Hence quality-of-life measurements could lead to proposals for preventive and rehabilitative procedures. McCartney and Larson provide a comprehensive list: patient education programmes, support groups, pain management techniques, preventive measures for anticipatory nausea with chemotherapy, medications for symptom control, and professional counselling about sexual function, family and marital relationships, or adjustment to terminal illness.

These interventions, they suggest, should be evaluated for costs and benefits, with accurate measures of outcomes required.

This example from the field of cancer illustrates that if health programmes are to be properly evaluated appropriate measures are needed: sometimes 'official' statistics will be sufficient, sometimes these will be necessary, for the task. In some circumstances entirely new measures will be required. The last 45 years have seen the development, as one consequence of these concerns for appropriate measures, of health status and quality-of-life measures to cope with the fundamental issues surrounding the quality of life, which for most people would include good health.

Technological Change

In medicine, as elsewhere, technological change has proceeded at a rapid and indeed bewildering pace this century, and especially since the Second World War. Haber (1986) presents a comprehensive taxonomy of technological change encompassing health care technology and 'ecological' technology. The health care category contains diagnostic devices and procedures, drugs, prosthetics, and biomaterials (e.g. implants). In this context Levine (in Mosteller *et al.*, 1989) talks of 'new and dramatic technologies' citing as examples organ transplantation, artificial organs, coronary artery bypass surgery, angioplasty and renal dialysis.

Also included in Haber's taxonomy, perhaps more controversially given one's 'everyday' perception of technology, are health services research – defined as new methods of delivering health care and of testing for effectiveness and cost-effectiveness – and 'biotelemetry': the transferring of information of biological importance from the patient to the physician or health care worker. Ecological technology encompasses activities of daily living (bathing, dressing, feeding, etc.), instrumental activities of daily living (shopping, cooking, etc.), transportation and mobility, communications, workplace design and recreation.

The key point to be made here is that technological change needs to be monitored. Clearly if new machines improve diagnosis, for example, we would want to see if such improvements justify the cost of adopting the new technology. If new ways of undertaking medical care save or extend lives these outcomes can be measured. If health status and quality of life is going to be changed by new technology then we need measures of health status and quality of life.

At the same time we may wish to curb the over-enthusiastic application of new technology. This was neatly illustrated in a TV programme in which a doctor stated: 'When someone gets a new hammer everything begins to look like a nail.' The context was a discussion of sports medicine, where the doctor felt that too much use was being made of arthroscopy and that alternatives such as rehabilitation and conservative therapy were more appropriate. Here again it can be argued that health status and quality of life are at issue in the potential implementation of a new technique and so their measurement may help resource allocation decisions to be made in such a case.

It is apparent from this discussion that technology, health status and the quality of life go together: if more people live and life is prolonged for the survivors through the agency of technological change then the quality of life is undoubtedly a key matter.

We should not of course lose sight, in emphasising the need for health status and quality of life measurement, of the fact that new technology often does not come cheaply. Indeed one of the major reasons for the dramatic increases in health care costs in most countries – with widely differing health sector structures and financing patterns – is the cost of technological change, often associated with the rapid pace of this change. Another major reason is demographic change, in the shape of ageing populations. Taking these two features together it will be apparent that the gains in life expectancy at the aggregate level from new technology and medical interventions more generally are becoming increasingly marginal. Given this, quality-of-life considerations assume greater importance in the evaluation of medical and health-related activity.

Medical Effectiveness

It can come as something of a surprise to a non-medical layperson that the effectiveness of many medical interventions is open to question. If we say an intervention or procedure is effective we mean that it 'works' – giving a person or more generally a group of persons a course of drugs, say, leads to a distinct improvement in health, an improvement that would not be obtained by not administering the drug. (Clearly other interventions may also deliver improvements for the same disease condition, so that the relative effectiveness of alternative interventions would then be under consideration.)

At one extreme of the controversy over the value of medical practice we should perhaps place Illich (1975), who was scathing about the value of medical interventions. Apart from dealing with the trauma caused by accidents, medical interventions are useless or, worse, harmful. The term 'iatrogenic disease' became a part of the vocabulary, as did 'DOMPS' (the diseases of medical progress), in discussing this issue. In the face of such views it is clearly important to take seriously the question of the risks and benefits of all kinds of medical and health interventions.

The key to the assessment of medical effectiveness is rigorous evaluation of the outcomes. One way of approaching this is the randomised controlled trial: the relationships between this approach, health status measurement, and decision-making are treated in Chapter 6. There is no doubt that uncertainty and disagreement do exist in the medical profession over the role of many common practices. This is reflected, for example, in large variations in therapeutic practices among doctors, and large variations in the frequency of application of medical procedures. Wennberg and his colleagues (1980) assessed nine different surgical procedures – hysterectomy, tonsillectomy, repair of inguinal hernia, cholecystectomy, prostatectomy, extraction of lens for cataract, caesarian section, appendectomy, hemorrhoidectomy – for which they evaluated resource costs and surgery-associated deaths. On the basis of their study they suggested that: *(i)* clear information on the risks and expected gains of alternative methods of treatment does not exist as part of a systematic accepted body of scientific knowledge, and *(ii)* expected outcomes of medical choices are unclear and cannot be anticipated with certainty by either doctors or patients. In a later paper Eddy and Billings (1988) stated: 'for at least some important practices, the existing evidence is of such poor quality that it is virtually impossible to determine even what effect the practice has on patients, much less whether that effect is preferable to the outcomes that would have occurred with other options.'

The whole area of what is now being termed *medical practice variations* is the subject of a book in the present series (Andersen and Mooney, 1990). The editors themselves boldly assert: 'Substantial variations in utilisation of modern medical care seem to be more of an overwhelming rule than an exceptional phenomenon.' One of the messages from this book is the need for systematic outcomes research and evaluation, which clearly could include health status and quality-of-life measurement, the concerns of the present volume.

Indeed this was concluded a decade earlier by Wennberg and his colleagues. They suggested that, first, special attention should be paid to the valuation of quality of life subsequent to medical intervention and, second, there should be substantial public investment in the assessment of the outcomes of common medical and surgical practices and the value of health care technology.

Organisational and Finance Changes

It would be difficult to find a country in the so-called 'developed' world in which there has been no agonising over what is often termed the 'explosion' in health care costs in recent times. This concern about the amounts of expenditure incurred in the health sector applies right across the board, from allegedly relatively 'low' spenders, such as the UK, to the 'high' spenders, in particular the USA. And the concern occurs for a wide variety of health systems, organisational and financial. The term 'rationing' is being used with ever greater frequency in health sector debates. To economists the explicit consideration now given to this notion has been a welcome development. For perhaps too long, discussion of the use of resources in health has been conducted along the somewhat unreal lines that the only thing wrong is that health services are 'underfunded'. This may be the case, but it has to be demonstrated! Health status and quality-of-life measurement may then be necessary components of the evaluation required to inform debate on organisation and financing.

Considerable efforts have been made, or are in train, to change or reorganise the ways in which health services are financed and delivered. In the UK, for example, the government has chosen to move towards a system of producer or internal markets, whilst substantially retaining the mainly public financing of the system. In the USA important developments involving new types of delivery systems such as Health Maintenance Organisations can be observed. In addition, resource allocation experiments such as that embarked upon in Oregon have provoked substantial controversy (see, for example, Hadorn, 1991, and Daniels, 1991). This is just one part of the substantial financing/health care organisation debate which is under way in the US, not least because President Clinton has made health a major priority.

Changes like these are partly, perhaps in some countries mainly, about controlling health care costs. But phrases like 'obtaining value for money' are commonly heard, not least from politicians. If the focus is not to be solely on reducing costs but truly on evaluation then serious attention has to be paid to the enumeration and evaluation of outcomes.

The term 'low spender' on health was used to characterise the UK, but clearly criteria are required to judge what is 'low' and what is 'high'. The ultimate goal of all spending is surely the happiness, well-being, welfare, call it what one may, of the members of the human race. We have to ask questions not only about the levels of spending on health (and anything else) in the achievement of this goal but also just how the available resources are being, or might be, used. Health status and quality of life measures may help us to answer such questions.

Cultural Developments

This catch-all phrase is used to suggest that there has been in recent years greater criticism of the biomedical model and greater scepticism of the value of health interventions. In part, of course, this reflects the problems over medical effectiveness and medical practice variations outlined above. Levine (in Mosteller *et al.*, 1989) suggests such criticism has come from women, minorities, and the holistic movement and that it points to 'the need to humanise services and pay more attention to the social functioning of patients'. These few sentences do scant justice to the seriousness with which these issues are taken, but certainly indicate that medical practice and health interventions do indeed have to be viewed within alternative social and cultural environments. Concern for these wider matters would again appear to justify the development of health status and quality-of-life measures which are the subject of this book.

Given the considerations that have been raised in this chapter we may summarise the reasons for studying health status and its measurement as:

1. Understanding the causes and consequences of differences in health.
2. Estimating the needs of populations.
3. Improving clinical decisions.
4. Assessing the quality of care.
5. Measuring the efficacy, effectiveness and efficiency of medical interventions.

A number of the issues treated briefly in this chapter will be given more extended treatment in subsequent chapters. Particular attention will be given to the changing context in which these issues arise.

CHAPTER 2
An Outline of the Development of Health Status Measures

Providing a history of the development of health status measures is not the most straightforward of tasks. In some ways the use of the term 'health status measure' is perhaps unhelpful since it suggests a rather narrow health-based focus. Any assessment of outcome measurement and, more generally, evaluation in health and medicine quickly leads one into a complex area populated by members of various disciplines and replete with terminologies that are not always as carefully defined as they might be. Some of the disciplines – in alphabetical order – are: economics, epidemiology, medicine, moral philosophy, political science, psychology, sociology and statistics. Amongst the terminologies are: health status indicators, indexes, measures and surveys; functional status, functional assessment; utility measurement; quality of life, and health-related quality of life. The last term has become particularly popular in the literature of health assessment. What researchers and practitioners seek are measures which capture people's ability to function or, rather more broadly, their well-being resulting from health programmes or interventions. The last 45 years or so have seen the burgeoning of such measures. It could be argued that in essence analysts have taken up the challenge of 'operationalising' the all-embracing WHO definition mentioned in Chapter 1.

Before considering how health status measurement has proceeded over time, we should outline the nature of the tasks involved in such measurement. In developing a health status measure essentially three steps are needed.

1. The choice and classification of dimensions and items for inclusion in the measure.
2. The 'scaling', measurement, or valuation of these dimensions and items.
3. Some ethically appropriate rule for aggregating the valuations arrived at during step 2.

It will be apparent that a set of distinctive tasks is to be accomplished. Initially there are the elements of classification and description. This can be a very instructive exercise because what appears in a measure and how the measure is structured must be carefully related to the objectives that are to be pursued. These objectives can of course differ so it should come as no surprise that a wide variety of measures have been developed, as will be shown below. The second set of tasks takes us to measurement: once we have a set of health state (or quality of life) 'descriptors' in place, these should be measured or valued in some way. Now the neat three-step scheme may have to be disturbed, because it may be argued that measurement and valuation should be logically separated. Thus there may be physical measures which represent the outcomes of medical interventions – people may move from a particular defined health state to another health state – but the further task is to evaluate such moves. Measurement is considered in more detail in Chapter 5.

The final task has caused a great deal of debate because we have to find a way or ways of aggregating individual valuations. Put this into the utility context of Chapter 1 and we find ourselves in a minefield. There arises, for example, the classic dilemma of interpersonal comparisons: how can the health status analyst be sure that your *perception* of a change in health state is the same as mine, or alternatively that it is different from mine, so that our utilities from medical interventions can be compared in any meaningful way? This is not mere academic 'point-scoring': the context may well be how to allocate substantial sums of money or resources, so that it is not sufficient merely to describe potential health status changes but some form of (social) evaluation must be accomplished. These basic issues will recur during the course of the book.

Bearing this framework in mind, how has health status measurement developed and what measures have been tried or are currently available? Rosser (1983) has traced the development of health indicators to the Laws of Hammurabi, inscribed in Babylon. From these she has derived a 'Utility Scale adjusted for socio-economic group' ranging from 10 – death of freeman/loss of eye of freeman/loss of hand of surgeon (for surgical failures) – to 2 – death of slave/loss of eye of slave – and 0.2: death of ox. This 'first heroic age of health indicators ended in 1750 BC'.

The 'second heroic age' commences in Britain with the Victorians and Florence Nightingale, aided and abetted by the formidable William Farr, who worked for 40 years at the General Register Office in London. At this juncture medical statisticians might want to put a word in for John Graunt (1662) who analysed the London Bills of Mortality, which were weekly compilations of deaths obtained by house-to-house visiting; and other anteceding pioneers might be cited. (Brief outlines of the history of medical statistics can be found in Logan and Lambert (1979) and Lancaster (1974)). Florence Nightingale, though, was concerned with what we might now call 'value for money': she wanted the sort of data that would allow her to show that there was 'great and unnecessary waste of life' in hospitals. Her outcome system was, simply, 'dead', 'relieved' or 'unrelieved', a system that was scarcely improved upon for decades. Her *Notes on Hospitals* (1863) can be regarded as the first initiative in Britain to introduce medical audit.

CLASSIFICATION OF HEALTH STATUS MEASURES

For the more modern developments we require some form of classification to bring shape to what can be a confusing picture. This classification is not the only way of categorising health status measurement but it should serve our purposes. A category of measure commonly entitled *functional assessment* can be discerned. Then there are what are called *generic* (or *general* or *global* or *multi-attribute* or *multi-dimensional*) measures which essentially take two forms: those of an *aggregate* nature (sometimes termed an 'index') and those which present health *profiles*. Further, some measures are termed *specific* instruments: these comprise disease-specific, function-specific, condition- or problem-specific, and population-specific. Included amongst this class of measures would be many of the mental health status measures that have been developed. Finally, and perhaps most closely within the economics tradition, are *utility* measures.

Now these categories are not necessarily mutually exclusive. Indeed the generic measures take their name precisely because they usually contain the dimensions of physical, emotional and social functioning which appear elsewhere in the functional and mental assessments. Similarly some authors have included utility measures under the generic heading. For convenience of exposition, however, we shall use the framework outlined.

Functional Assessment Measures

Katz (1983), a major figure in the construction of functional assessment measures, has provided a succinct account of developments in this field. He points out that information about functional status was obtained in health interview surveys in Europe and the United States in the late 1800s and early 1900s. These surveys were concerned with the prevalence of morbidity in large populations and included sickness data and information on ability to work. By the 1940s hierarchically ordered classifications of disability to reflect severity of illness had appeared and in the early 1950s a Canadian survey had in a limited sense combined inputs and outputs by the introduction of use: disability ratios such as days of hospitalisation per 100 days of disability (Dominion Bureau of Statistics, 1956). The 1950s saw a substantial expansion in the development of functional and disability measures and, in particular, the construction and use of activities of daily living (ADL) indices. Katz points to the problems with these early efforts: impracticality and poor reproducibility because of vague terminology, reliance on clinical impression (apparently this was generally unreliable about patients' functional potential), and the lack of meaningful bases for comparative weighting and scoring.

Given these weaknesses, substantial efforts were devoted to deriving measures which would be reliable, valid and useful. This emphasis on a 'sound' methodology does not only, of course, apply to functional assessment. Indeed it is so important right across the board of measurement that Chapter 3 will be devoted to an explanation of methodological criteria.

The development of functional assessment measures has been related to the concepts of impairment, disability and handicap. This is perhaps not surprising, since these measures were largely developed in the context of chronic diseases, geriatric medicine, and rehabilitation. The precise nature of the concepts has not been without controversy amongst writers on these matters, but the following definitions appear to command a reasonably wide level of agreement (see, for example, Wilkin et al., 1992). *Impairment* covers any disturbance of, or interference with, the normal structure and functioning of the body, including mental functions. *Disability* is the loss or reduction of functional ability and activity consequent upon impairment. *Handicap* reflects the value attached to an individual's status when this departs from the norm – this is related to some notion of social status or social functioning.

What came to be sought by some doctors were formal or standardised approaches to functional measurement. After all, doctors had been quite used to taking medical 'histories' from patients. How then to standardise measurement and to take on board the wider concerns about patient functioning, independence and so on were seen as tasks to be accomplished if medical care was to be improved. Some of the early functional instruments were rooted in the diagnostic tests and standardised medical summaries of a patient's condition, and the instruments or functional scales were usually administered by doctors or other medical personnel. As more emphasis came to be placed, for example in the context of rehabilitation, on the abilities of people to function independently and socially, the assessment of disability and handicap took more prominence: the development of *activities of daily living* scales reflected these concerns. Feinstein et al. (1986) have traced the concept of activities of daily living back to Sheldon in 1935, but suggest that the first published use of the term was by Buchwald in 1949.

Next the move to *instrumental activities of daily living* occurred, stimulated in part by the movement towards community care for the elderly. In anticipation of later material in this chapter we can discern the logic in moving even further – towards instruments or measures which attempt to capture social functioning via the concept of quality of life, that is, towards the development of generic measures.

Let us return to Katz (1983), who is especially appreciative of Lawton's (1972) behavioural model in which function is viewed within a hierarchy of domains, each of which includes a set of functions that can be ordered along a continuum from simple to complex. Put somewhat more simply (!) the 'domain of ADL' contains three components or dimensions: basic ADL, mobility, and instrumental ADL (IADL). Basic ADL items comprise: bathing, dressing, toileting, transfer, continence, feeding. IADL items include: shopping, cooking, housekeeping, laundry, use of transport, managing money, managing medication, and use of the telephone. Mobility can be of the IADL-type, e.g. use of transport, or something more basic, such as simply being able to get out of the house.

A variety of functional assessment measures has been compiled and used in a multiplicity of settings. Table 2.1 gives some indication of this variety. Examples of the coverage of some of these measures are given in Table 2.2. The Barthel, Kenny and Index of ADL are all examples of ADL measures. The FSI indicates the somewhat broader scope of the IADL approach: the interpersonal activities dimension comprises four items, namely: driving a car, visiting family or friends, attending meetings, and performing your job.

Typically the functional status measures contain questions concerning what we might call 'grades of performance' so that scores can be assigned to the persons under review or study. Thus the Index of ADL feeding items has three grades 'feeds self without assistance', 'feeds self except for getting assistance in cutting meat or buttering bread', and 'receives assistance in feeding or is fed partly or completely by using tubes or intravenous fluids'.

One obvious question which arises for anyone setting out to use one or more functional assessment method(s) is 'Which do we choose?' The answer will clearly depend on the purpose(s) at hand. An excellent guide to a number of functional assessment measures is provided in McDowell and Newell's (1987) book. Every instrument or measure or what the authors refer to as 'scales' (a terminology reserved in the present book for the scaling methods of measurement: see Chapter 5) is described and reviewed on a series of criteria. These are: the purpose of the measure; the conceptual basis, if any, for the measure; reliability; and validity. A brief commentary sums up the authors' views on each measure along with their recommendations on usage. Full or abbreviated versions of the instruments themselves are reproduced, along with the scoring systems employed. A similar service is performed by Wilkin *et al.* (1992).

It should be stated that McDowell and Newell are quite critical about various aspects of the development of ADL measures. First, this development has been uncoordinated. Second, the definition of disability seems to have been taken for granted rather than explicitly stated. Third: 'There is no evidence for an accumulation of a body of scientific knowledge concerning the concept of disability, its relationship to impairment and handicap, or of the sequence in which changes in disability occur as a patient's condition deteriorates or improves.' Fourth, little is known about the overlap between the various instruments and not enough comparative work on the instruments

Table 2.1 Functional assessment instruments

Instrument	Reference
Katz ADL	Katz et al. (1963)
PULSES	Moskowitz and McCann (1957)
Modified ADL Scales	Katz and Akpom (1976)
Kenny Self-Care Evaluation	Schoening and Iversen (1968)
Barthel Index	Mahoney and Barthel (1965)
Rapid Disability Rating Scale	Linn and Linn (1982)
PACE 11	US DHEW (1978)
Performance ADL (PADL)	Kuriansky and Gurland (1976)
Functional Health Scale	Rosow and Breslow (1966)
Functional Activities Questionnaire	Pfeffer et al. (1982)
Comprehensive Assessment and Referral Evaluation (CARE)	Gurland et al. (1977)
MAI (Multilevel Assessment Instrument)	Lawton et al. (1982)
Functional Life Scale	Sarno et al. (1973)
Long Range Evaluation Summary	Granger (1982)
Northwick Park	Sheikh et al. (1979)
Rivermead	Whiting et al. (1980)
Index of Nursing Dependency	Smith et al. (1977)
McClatchie	McClatchie et al. (1983)
Functional Assessment Inventory	Pfeiffer et al. (1981)
Patient Status Instrument	Weissert et al. (1979)
Fugl-Meyer and Jääskö	Fugl-Meyer and Jääskö (1980)
Level of Rehabilitation Scale (LORS)	Trudel et al. (1984)
Convery Polyarticular Disability Index	Convery et al. (1977)
Ceder	Ceder and Thorngren (1982)
Comprehensive Older Persons Evaluation (COPE)	Pearlman (1987)
Functional Status Index (FSI)	Jette et al. (1980)
Patient Evaluation Conference System	Harvey and Jellinek (1981)
The Lambeth Disability Screening Questionnaire	Charlton et al. (1983)
Disability and Impairment Interview Schedule	Garrad and Bennett (1971)
Physical Self Maintenance Scale	Lawton and Brody (1969)
The Functional Status Rating System	Forer (1981)
OECD Long-Term Disability Questionnaire	McWhinnie (1981)

Table 2.2 Functional assessment measures: some examples of coverage

Barthel	Feeding, grooming, transfer, toileting, bathing, walking/locomotion, continence.
Functional Status Index (FSI)	Mobility, hand activities, personal care, home chores, interpersonal activities.
Index of ADL	Bathing, dressing, toileting, transfer, continence, feeding.
Kenny	Bed activities, transfers, locomotion, continence, dressing, feeding.

An Outline of the Development of Health Status Measures

has been accomplished. Finally, a large number of measures have inadequate evidence of reliability and validity. These concepts will be explained in the next chapter.

These authors' views on IADLs are kinder: they believe that these measures have been more thoroughly tested, particularly with respect to reliability and validity, and are more sensitive to minor variations in a patient's condition. There still remains, however, the problem of compatibility across instruments. They judge that the broader IADL approach will tend to supplant the older ADL methods, even in the context of clinical studies. They are also of the opinion that the IADL measures in their turn will be replaced by the even more comprehensive general health status measures.

This is nicely borne out by the Functional Status Questionnaire (FSQ) (Jette *et al.*, 1986). Although its title suggests that it is a functional assessment measure, its dimensions ('functions' in Jette's terminology) encompass physical, psychological and social/role, along with additional single item questions (see Figure 2.1). The functional status report which is generated from the questionnaire replies is also reproduced (Figure 2.2). By developing the earlier FSI into the more comprehensive FSQ, Jette and his colleagues would thus appear to have produced a more generic measure. We can now turn our attention to the generic approach.

Generic Measures

Aggregate

As we have just seen, the functional assessment measures, especially in the form of ADL measures, have their limitations. For these and other reasons, researchers became more ambitious in their attempts at capturing the nature of health status and, beyond this, the whole range of physical, mental and social functioning. Now, although it can be judged that some of the measures usually classified as functional assessment measures do cover this range, several determined attempts were made to develop summary or global concepts such as a 'well-year'. Pioneers in this work, dating back to the early 1970s, were Bush and his colleagues (see, for example, Kaplan, Bush and Berry, 1976). Later workers have referred to the Bush measure as the 'Rolls-Royce' of such measures. If the Rolls-Royce is a complex machine, the same could probably be said of the Bush index! The key features in the construction of this index are four attributes, namely mobility, physical function, social function and 'symptom-problem complex'. The incorporation of functional measures gives a clear link with the ADL/functional assessment work. Bush's team defined 43 function levels and 36 symptom-problem complexes. Using these concepts the Quality of Well-Being (QWB) could be measured for the individual and 'well-years' could be calculated and aggregated across

Figure 2.1 Functional status questionnaire

Category	Item
Physical function: During the past month have you had difficulty:	
Basic activities of daily living (ADL)	Taking care of yourself, that is eating, dressing or bathing?
	Moving in and out of a bed or chair?
	Walking indoors, such as around your home?
Intermediate ADL	Walking several blocks?
	Walking one block or climbing one flight of stairs?
	Doing work around the house such as cleaning, light yard work, home maintenance?
	Doing errands, such as grocery shopping?
	Driving a car or using public transportation?
	Doing vigorous activities such as running, lifting heavy objects or participating in strenuous sports?

Responses: usually did with no difficulty (4), some difficulty (3), much difficulty (2), usually did not because of health (1), usually did not do for other reasons (0).

Psychological function: During the past month:	
Mental health	Have you been a very nervous person?
	Have you felt calm and peaceful?*
	Have you felt downhearted and blue?
	Were you a happy person?*
	Did you feel so down in the dumps that nothing could cheer you up?

Responses: all of the time (1), most of the time (2), a good bit of the time (3), some of the time (4), a little of the time (5), none of the time (6).

Social role function: During the past month have you:	
Work performance (for those employed, during the preceding month)	Done as much work as others in similar jobs?*
	Worked for short periods of time or taken frequent rests because of your health?
	Worked your regular number of hours?*
	Done your job as carefully and accurately as others with similar jobs?*
	Worked at your usual job, but with some changes because of your health?
	Feared losing your job because of your health?

Responses: all of the time (1), most of the time (2), some of the time (3), none of the time (4).

Social activity	Had difficulty visiting with relatives or friends?
	Had difficulty participating in community activities, such as religious services, social activities, or volunteer work?
	Had difficulty taking care of other people such as family members?

Responses: usually did with no difficulty (4), some difficulty (3), much difficulty (2), usually did not do because of health (1), usually did not do for other reasons (0).

Quality of interaction	Isolated yourself from people around you?
	Acted affectionate toward others?*
	Acted irritable towards those around you?
	Made unreasonable demands on your family and friends?
	Gotten along well with other people?*

Responses: all of the time (1), most of the time (2), a good bit of the time (3), some of the time (4), a little of the time (5), none of the time (6).

Single item questions:
Which of the following statements best describes your work situation during the past month?
Responses: working full-time; working part-time: unemployed, looking for work: unemployed because of my health: retired because of my health: retired for some other reason.

During the past month, how many days did illness or injury keep you in bed all or most of the day?
Response: 0–31 days.

During the past month, how many days did you cut down on the things you usually do for one-half day or more because of your own illness or injury?
Response: 0–31 days.

During the past month, how satisfied were you with your sexual relationships?
Responses: very satisfied, satisfied, not sure, dissatisfied, very dissatisfied, did not have any sexual relationships.

How do you feel about your own health?
Responses: very satisfied, satisfied, not sure, dissatisfied, very dissatisfied.

During the past month, about how often did you get together with friends or relatives, such as going out together, visiting in each other's homes, or talking on the telephone?
Responses: every day, several times a week, about once a week, two or three times a month, about once a month, not at all.

* Scores are reversed.

Source: Jette et al. (1986).

Figure 2.2 Functional status report: sample

	(Warning Zone = ...)	
Physical function		
Basic activities of daily living (ADL)	0 .... 56 _____	100
Intermediate ADL	0 .... 7 _____	100
Psychological function		
Mental health	0 .... 36 _____	100
Role function		
Employment status	Retired because of health	
Work performance	Not applicable	
Social function		
Social activity	0 0 _____	100
Quality of interaction	0 .... 56 _____	100
Frequency of contact	Every day	
Bed days	0	
Restricted days	31	
Sexual relationships	Did not have any sexual relationships	
Feeling about health	Very dissatisfied	

Summary
The patient scored in the acceptable range of the following scales: none.
Responses to the functional status questionnaire reveal the following general areas of concern: basic activities of daily living, intermediate activities of daily living, mental health, social activity, quality of interaction.
The patient reported significant problems with the following activities: eat/dress/bathe, walk one block, work around the house, do errands, drive a car, visit relatives or friends, community activities, take care of other people, vigorous activities.

* A higher score means better functional ability.

Source: Jelte et al., 1986.

individuals. How were these calculations accomplished?

The index places each individual into one of 43 mutually exclusive and collectively exhaustive levels of functioning, these levels being obtained from 3 separate scales of functioning, namely: mobility, physical activity, and social activity; see Table 2.3 for a list of these function levels. In addition each person is classified according to the symptom or problem that bothers him/her the most, there being 36 such complexes of symptoms or problems: these are listed in Table 2.4. By adjusting the score obtained from the patient on functioning and symptom/problem for the social preference or weight for the patient's particular condition, the individual can be placed at a point on the scale 1.0 (optimum function) to 0.0 (death). We shall return to the question of determining social weights shortly, but first let us look at some illustrative numbers. Suppose an individual has a health state value calculated in the way just described at 0.50 prior to medical intervention and 0.57 after some intervention. If this difference of 0.07 is maintained for one year the 'production' of well-years is 0.07 well-years. If this benefit accrued for 100 people, total benefit would be 7.00 well-years. This benefit, it is claimed, can then be compared with cost, and the benefits of alternative programmes be compared with the costs of these programmes. Note that this method would now be placed under the rubric of cost-utility analysis, rather than cost-benefit analysis, should the latter term be reserved for evaluation of both costs and benefits in monetary terms, as present convention usually suggests.

It is not proposed to provide a critique of this sort of approach to the measurement of health status at this juncture. What we will do, however, is to point out the salient features of the approach. Note first the attempt to be comprehensive – the examples shown in Tables 2.3 and 2.4 indicate this. Hence the term 'generic' for this type of measure. Typically in developing such measures workers initially go for a large number of 'descriptors' or characterisations of physical, mental and social functioning and then try to find what they consider the minimum number of descriptors consistent with what they are seeking. This minimum number will require to fulfil criteria such as reliability, validity, responsiveness, reproducibility, practicality and so on. We consider the nature of these criteria in Chapter 3 but suffice it to say that at the very least health status measures should actually be measuring what they purport to measure! Thus, to indicate one potential dilemma, are there too many items/descriptors in the Bush measure, or too few? Answering 'too many' would imply that the measure is unnecessarily comprehensive, involves 'double counting', or is unduly complex for the purpose at hand. Answering 'too few' would imply perhaps that the index is not comprehensive enough to capture health status in a reliable and valid manner.

The second feature is the attempt to come up with a single score. This has clear advantages in terms of providing a 'summary' measure of health status. Essentially it allows quantitative comparisons to be made between

Table 2.3 The Bush index: function levels and associated levels of well-being

Function level number (1)	Scale			Level of well-being (W_j)
	Mobility	Physical activity	Social activity	
	NO SYMPTOM PROBLEM COMPLEX			
L43	Drove car and used bus or train without help (5)	Walked without physical problems (4)	Did work, school, or housework, and other activities (5)	1.000
	SYMPTOM/PROBLEM COMPLEX PRESENT			
L42	Drove car and used bus or train without help (5)	Walked without physical problems (4)	Did work, school, or housework, and other activities (5)	0.7433
L41	Drove car and used bus or train without help (5)	Walked without physical problems (4)	Did work, school, or housework, but other activities limited (4)	0.6855
L40	Drove car and used bus or train without help (5)	Walked without physical problems (4)	Limited in amount or kind of work, school, or housework (3)	0.6683
L39	Drove car and used bus or train without help (5)	Walked without physical problems (4)	Performed self-care, but not work, school, or housework (2)	0.6955
L38	Drove car and used bus or train without help (5)	Walked without physical problems (4)	Had help with self-care activities (1)	0.6370
L37	Drove car and used bus or train without help (5)	Walked with physical limitations (3)	Did work, school, or housework, and other activities (5)	0.6769
L36	Drove car and used bus or train without help (5)	Walked with physical limitations (3)	Did work, school, or housework, but other activities limited (4)	0.6172
L35	Drove car and used bus or train without help (5)	Walked with physical limitations (3)	Limited in amount or kind of work, school, or housework (3)	0.6020
L34	Drove car and used bus or train without help (5)	Walked with physical limitations (3)	Performed self-care, but not work, school, or housework (2)	0.6292
L33	Drove car and used bus or train without help (5)	Walked with physical limitations (3)	Had help with self-care activities (1)	0.5707

continued on page 26

Table 2.3 *continued*

Function level number (1)	Scale			Level of well-being
	Mobility	Physical activity	Social activity	(W_j)
L32	Did not drive, or had help to use bus or train (4)	Walked without physical problems (4)	Did work, school, or housework but other activities limited (4)	0.6065
L31	Did not drive, or had help to use bus or train (4)	Walked without physical problems (4)	Limited in amount or kind of work, school, or housework (3)	0.5913
L30	Did not drive, or had help to use bus or train (4)	Walked without physical problems (4)	Performed self-care, but not work, school, or housework (2)	0.6185
L29	Did not drive, or had help to use bus or train (4)	Walked without physical problems (4)	Had help with self-care activities (1)	0.5600
L28	Did not drive, or had help to use bus or train (4)	Walked with physical limitations (3)	Did work, school, or housework, but other activities limited (4)	0.5402
L27	Did not drive, or had help to use bus or train (4)	Walked with physical limitations (3)	Limited in amount or kind of work, school, or housework (3)	0.5250
L26	Did not drive, or had help to use bus or train (4)	Walked with physical limitations (3)	Performed self-care, but not work, school, or housework (2)	0.5523
L25	Did not drive, or had help to use bus or train (4)	Moved own wheelchair without help (2)	Limited in amount or kind of work, school, or housework (3)	0.5376
L24	Did not drive, or had help to use bus or train (4)	Moved own wheelchair without help (2)	Performed self-care, but not work, school, or housework (2)	0.5649
L23	In house (3)	Walked without physical problems (4)	Performed self-care, but not work, school, or housework (2)	0.6488
L22	In house (3)	Walked without physical problems (4)	Had help with self-care activities (1)	0.5902
L21	In house (3)	Walked with physical limitations (3)	Did work, school, or housework, but other activities limited (4)	0.5704
L20	In house (3)	Walked with physical	Limited in amount or kind of	0.5552

L19	In house (3)	Walked with physical limitations (3)	work, school, or housework (3) Performed self-care, but not work, school, or housework (2)	0.5824
L18	In house (3)	Walked with physical limitations (3)	Had help with self-care activities (1)	0.5239
L17	In house (3)	Moved own wheelchair without help (2)	Performed self care, but not work, school, or housework (2)	0.5950
L16	In house (3)	Moved own wheelchair without help (2)	Had help with self care activities (1)	0.5364
L15	In house (3)	In bed or chair (1)	Performed self care, but not work, school, or housework (2)	0.5715
L14	In house (3)	In bed or chair (1)	Had help with self-care activities (1)	0.5129
L13	In hospital (2)	Walked without physical problems (4)	Performed self care, but not work, school, or housework (2)	0.6057
L12	In hospital (2)	Walked without physical problems (4)	Had help with self-care activities (1)	0.5471
L11	In hospital (2)	Walked with physical limitations (3)	Performed self-care, but not work, school, or housework (2)	0.5394
L10	In hospital (2)	Walked with physical limitations (3)	Had help with self-care activities (1)	0.4808
L 9	In hospital (2)	Moved own wheelchair without help (2)	Performed self-care, but not work, school, or housework (2)	0.5520
L 8	In hospital (2)	Moved own wheelchair without help (2)	Had help with self-care activities (1)	0.4934
L 7	In hospital (2)	In bed or chair (1)	Performed self-care, but not work, school, or housework (2)	0.5284
L 6	In hospital (2)	In bed or chair (1)	Had help with self-care activities (1)	0.4699
L 5	In special care unit (1)	Walked without physical problems (4)	Performed self-care, but not work, school, or housework (2)	0.5732

continued on page 28

Table 2.3 continued

Function level number (1)	Scale			Level of well-being (W_j)
	Mobility	Physical activity	Social activity	
L 4	In special care unit (1)	Walked without physical problems (4)	Had help with self-care activities (1)	0.5147
L 3	In special care unit (1)	Walked with physical limitations (3)	Performed self-care, but not work, school, or housework (2)	0.5070
L 2	In special care unit (1)	Walked with physical limitations (3)	Had help with self-care activities (1)	0.4483
L 1	In special care unit (1)	In bed or chair (1)	Had help with self-care activities (1)	0.4374
L 0	Dead (0)	Dead (0)	Dead (0)	0.0000

Source: Kaplan *et al.*, 1976.

An Outline of the Development of Health Status Measures

Table 2.4 The Bush index: symptom-problem complexes

Symptom–Problem Complex	Adjustment
1. Trouble seeing (includes wearing glasses or contacts).	.01898
2. Pain or discomfort in one or both eyes, such as burning or itching.	.03370
3. Trouble hearing (includes wearing hearing aid).	.08338
4. Earache, toothache, or pain in jaw.	.09779
5. Sore throat, lips, tongue, gums or stuffy, runny nose.	.09332
6. Several or all permanent teeth missing or crooked.	.07154
7. Pain, bleeding, itching, or discharge (drainage) from sexual organs (excludes normal menstruation).	−.09202
8. Itching, bleeding, or pain in rectum.	−.03795
9. Pain in chest, stomach, side, back or hips.	−.03824
10. Cough *and* fever or chills.	.00775
11. Cough, wheezing, or shortness of breath.	−.00752
12. Sick or upset stomach, vomiting, or diarrhoea (watery bowel movements).	.00655
13. Fever or chills with aching all over *and* vomiting or diarrhoea (watery bowel movements).	−.07216
14. Hernia or rupture of abdomen (stomach).	−.05008
15. Painful, burning, or frequent urination (passing water).	−.03271
16. Headache, dizziness, or ringing in ears.	.01308
17. Spells of feeling hot, nervous, or shaky.	.01288
18. Weak or deformed (crooked) back.	−.04743
19. Pain, stiffness, numbness, or discomfort of neck, hands, feet, arms, legs, or several joints.	−.03439
20. One *arm and one leg* deformed (crooked), paralysed (unable to move), or broken (includes wearing artificial limbs or braces).	−.06814
21. One *hand or arm* missing, deformed (crooked), paralysed (unable to move), or broken (includes wearing artificial limbs or braces).	−.06087
22. One *foot or leg* missing, deformed (crooked), paralysed (unable to move), or broken (includes wearing artificial limbs or braces).	−.06304
23. *Two legs* deformed (crooked), paralysed (unable to move), or broken (includes wearing artificial limbs or braces).	−.08806
24. *Two legs* missing (includes wearing artificial limbs or braces).	−.10270
25. Skin defect of face, arms or legs, such as scars, pimples, warts, bruises, or changes in colour.	.06331
26. Burning or itching rash on large areas of face, body, arms, or legs.	.01706
27. Burn over large areas of face, body, arms, or legs.	−.11004
28. Overweight for age and height.	.07848
29. General tiredness, weakness, or weight loss.	−.00270
30. Trouble talking, such as lisp, stuttering, hoarseness, or being unable to speak.	.01936
31. Trouble learning, remembering, or thinking clearly.	−.08298
32. Loss of consciousness such as seizures (fits), fainting or coma (out cold or knocked out).	−.15066
33. Taking medication or staying on prescribed diet for health reasons.	.11238
34. Breathing smog or unpleasant air.	.15553
35. No symptom or problem.	.25672
36. Spells of feeling upset, depressed, or crying.	

Source: Kaplan *et al.*, 1976.

health outcomes and resource use in obtaining these outcomes. Thus the techniques of cost-effectiveness analysis and cost-utility analysis could incorporate and make use of such single-score measures. Notice also that the method allows the comparison of health status changes between individuals and indeed allows health status to be added and subtracted, both for individuals and in the aggregate. Aggregation can, in principle, be at any level – diagnostic group, hospital patients, town, region, or nation.

Third, the method involves the incorporation of social preferences or weights. This is a distinctive feature of recent efforts to measure health status: we see here an attempt to accomplish the second step (and perhaps the third step) of health status measurement as described at the outset of this chapter, that is the *valuation* of health status. Bush and his colleagues calculated their social weights by taking random samples of citizens from the community. The question of whose values should be used in the scaling process is a controversial one: we shall return to it in Chapter 5.

Once these social weights are determined then if an individual is judged to be 'in' a particular health state then his/her responses to the functional assessment/symptom-problem questions will be adjusted by the social weighting given to this health state, as briefly outlined above. This means in effect that the individual's health status has been given a social valuation. Note also that the well-years calculated using the Bush method are to be treated as social valuations.

Another interesting attempt to develop an aggregate measure, influential in the British health status arena, is that of Rosser and Kind (1978). Rosser originally developed her health state descriptors by asking various groups of doctors to describe the criteria they used to judge the severity of illness in patients. From this work two principal components of severity emerged: namely, observed disability (loss of function and mobility) and subjective distress. The classification of illness states is reproduced as Table 2.5. A valuation matrix for these states was derived by using structured interviews (lasting anything between one-and-a-half and four hours) with 70 raters using a form of magnitude estimation scaling method, (see Chapter 5 for a description of this method). These 70 respondents comprised groups of medical patients, psychiatric patients, medical nurses, psychiatric nurses, healthy volunteers and doctors. The results are shown in Table 2.6. Note again that these weights can be regarded as 'social' and the resulting scores can be used in the derivation of quality-adjusted life-years. (QALYS).

Detailed advice on how to calculate QALYs using the Rosser method is provided in Gudex and Kind (1988). It is of interest to note that actually applying the method with particular groups of patients is quite straightforward, involving a three-page self-administered questionnaire which takes about ten minutes to complete. The results from the questionnaire classify patients into the cells of the distress–disability matrix (Table 2.5) and the weights (Table 2.6) are then applied for QALY purposes. QALYs have come to play

An Outline of the Development of Health Status Measures

Table 2.5 Rosser's classification of illness states

Disability		Distress
I	No disability	A. No distress
II	Slight social disability	B. Mild
III	Severe social disability and/or slight impairment of performance at work	C. Moderate
	Able to do all housework except very heavy tasks	D. Severe
IV	Choice of work or performance at work very severely limited	
	Housewives and old people able to do light housework only but able to go out shopping	
V	Unable to undertake any paid employment	
	Unable to continue any education	
	Old people confined to home except for escorted outings and short walks and unable to do shopping	
	Housewives able only to perform a few simple tasks	
VI	Confined to chair or to wheelchair or able to move around in the house only with support from an assistant	
VII	Confined to bed	
VIII	Unconscious	

Source: Gudex and Kind, 1988.

Table 2.6 Rosser's valuation matrix for 70 respondents

	Distress			
Disability	A	B	C	D
I	1.000	0.995	0.990	0.967
II	0.990	0.986	0.973	0.932
III	0.980	0.972	0.956	0.912
IV	0.964	0.956	0.942	0.870
V	0.946	0.935	0.900	0.700
VI	0.875	0.845	0.680	0.000
VII	0.677	0.564	0.000	−1.486
VIII	−1.028	−	−	−

Fixed points: Healthy = 1 Dead = 0

Source: Gudex and Kind, 1988.

a prominent part in recent developments in health status measurement, so more detailed consideration of the concept is presented in Chapters 5 and 7. Kind and his co-workers have continued to work with the Rosser approach: new matrices incorporating the values of a different sample of raters and using the scaling techniques of category rating, magnitude estimation, and the time trade-off, have been constructed (Gudex and Kind, 1993). Meanwhile Rosser and her colleagues at the Middlesex Hospital have designed a new Index of Health-Related Quality of Life (IHQL) which incorporates three dimensions, namely disability, distress and discomfort/pain (Rosser *et al.*, 1993).

An attempt to provide a truly international focus for health status measurement has been one of the goals of the Euroqol Group (The Euroqol Group, 1990). This is a multi-centre, five-country effort which is using a common questionnaire of the generic (index) variety. Further details of the approach are given in the context of scaling in Chapter 5.

Developing comprehensive aggregate measures is not straightforward, usually involving substantial research costs: this is perhaps indicated by the relative paucity of such measures (see Table 2.7).

Profiles

Profiles do not usually provide a single score but a set of profiles for each patient. Patients' profiles can then be clustered by, for example, disease or condition group. This would be of particular interest for evaluation and the possible resource allocation consequences of medical interventions. However the presentation of outcomes in profile form does not permit the cost/QALY type of calculation, so the usefulness of the profile approach in evaluation has been called into question. Nevertheless the profile approach has been quite extensively applied in the clinical environment and it clearly has its merits as a provider of ordered information on health status and quality of life.

An early example of the attempts to develop a generic measure is the Sickness Impact Profile (Bergner *et al.*, 1981). The profile originated in the belief that the aims of health care are to reduce sickness and its effects upon daily living. The basic objective was to construct a measure which was less sensitive to cultural variation and demographic limitations. Hence work began in 1972 on a measure that could be applied to a large number of conditions and across many locations. Following a series of 1108 field trials a prototype instrument was constructed comprising 312 items grouped into 14 dimensions. This was finally reduced to a more manageable format of 136 items under 12 dimensions covering such areas as work, recreation, emotional behaviour, social interaction, etc. (see Table 2.8). Three of the 12 dimensions may be used to form a physical score and 5 to form a psychosocial score. The questionnaire items took the form of statements such as: 'I have

Table 2.7 Generic measures: aggregate

Measure	Features		Score
Bush (Kaplan, 1982)	4 **Attributes:** mobility physical function social function symptom-problem complex	43 function levels 36 symptom-problem complex	Quality of well-being (QWB) for individual: 'well-years' can be aggregated
Rosser-Kind (Kind *et al.*, 1982)	2 **Dimensions:** distress disability	29 states	utility scales/states for individuals, can be aggregated
Wolfson (Wolfson *et al.* 1982)	10 **Functional categories** dressing, bathing, continence, eating, understanding, speech, wheelchair, transfer, ambulation, mental status	54 items	weighted index for individual, aggregated for group
Torrance (Torrance, 1982)	4 **Attributes** physical function role function social-emotional function health problem	23 items	individual utility function aggregated to group utility function
Euroqol (Williams, 1993)	5 **Dimensions** mobility self-care usual activities pain/discomfort anxiety/depression	15 items (243 possible combinations)	health states, can be scaled, aggregated

difficulty reasoning and problem solving' or 'I don't walk at all'. The items were weighted in accordance with the judgements of over 100 raters, who valued each item on an equal-interval 11-point scale ranging from minimal to severe dysfunction. The SIP score is derived by adding the scale values for each item, checking these values across all dimensions, dividing by the maximum possible dysfunction score for all dimensions and then multiplying by 100 to obtain the generic SIP value.

The SIP has been quite widely used: it has been translated into several different languages, including Spanish and Swedish, and has been used in a number of countries. In the United Kingdom the SIP has been reworked as the Functional Limitations Profile (FLP) (Patrick and Peach, 1989). The same format of 136 items in 12 dimensions was retained, but these items were reworded, reordered, and weighted using British raters. This SIP story

Table 2.8 Health profiles: an outline

Measure	Dimensions	Number of items
Sickness Impact Profile (Bergner et al., 1981)	12 sleep and rest, work, eating, mobility, home management, recreation and politics, body care and movement, ambulation, communication, social interaction, alertness behaviour, emotional behaviour	136
McMaster Health Index Questionnaire (Chambers et al., 1982)	3 physical function, emotional function, social function	59
Duke-UNC Profile (Parkerson et al., 1981)	4 symptom status, physical function, emotional function, social function	63
Nottingham Health Profile (McEwen, 1983)	13 physical mobility, pain, sleep, energy, social isolation, emotional reactions, employment, social life, household work, sex life, home life, holidays, interests and hobbies	45
Rand Health Insurance Study (Ware et al., 1984)	4 physical and role functioning, mental health, social contacts, general health perceptions	88
COOP Charts (Nelson et al., 1987)	9 physical, mental, role, social, pain, overall health change, overall health, social resources, life quality	9
SF-36 (Ware and Sherbourne, 1992)	8 physical functioning, vitality, social functioning, bodily pain, general mental health, general health perceptions, role limitations – physical, role limitations – emotional	36
OARS-MFAQ (Fillenbaum, 1988)	7 basic demographic, social resources, economic resources, mental health, physical health, activities of daily living, informant assessments	82

is an interesting one on account of these developments, illustrating as it does some of the discernible trends in health status measurement.

Clearly the SIP is a very lengthy instrument. This is one reason why its application in the clinical and care settings has been called into question by commentators such as McDowell and Newell (1987) and Wilkin et al. (1992). It should be stated, however, that independent observers such as these authors give the measure relatively high marks on methodological grounds. Later developments with other profiles have usually seen a reduction in the number of items assessed in questionnaires, partly in order to make their measures more applicable in the clinical setting. An example is the Duke-UNC (DUHP) profile (Parkerson et al., 1981): this 63-item instrument has been reduced to the 17-item Duke profile (Parkerson et al., 1990). Care has to be taken in item reduction to retain the sound methodological features of a lengthy instrument such as the SIP.

A profile which has achieved some popularity in the British context is the Nottingham Health Profile (NHP) (McEwen, 1983). A two-part questionnaire is used in which 45 yes/no questions are asked. Part I contains 6 dimensions – physical mobility, pain, sleep, energy, social isolation and emotional reactions. Part II broadens out into the dimensions of employment, social life, household work, home life, sex life, interests and hobbies, and holidays. The developers of the NHP came up initially with 2200 health state descriptors. Over a number of years of experimentation these were reduced to the 45 items shown here. This corresponds with a similar process in the construction of the SIP. The NHP has not been as well received as the SIP from the methodological standpoint (Kind and Carr-Hill, 1987; Wilkin et al., 1992), but its relative simplicity probably accounts for some of its popularity in the clinical environment.

A summary of the health profiles on offer is shown in Table 2.8.

Specific Measures

There is, as might be expected, a variety of these measures. Many of them are very similar in design and content to the functional assessment measures. Patrick and Deyo (1989) point out that disease-specific measures, for example, are designed to assess specific diagnostic groups or patient populations and are particularly aimed at measuring changes that may be of clinical importance for the practitioners concerned. Not all measures are disease-specific as such, but may be for specific groups such as the elderly, or disabled children.

Guyatt and his colleagues (1986) have shown how to develop disease-specific quality-of-life measures and, as will be observed in Table 2.9, it is possible to go for a Rolls-Royce design or a Volkswagen design! Table 2.10 presents a wide selection of the available measures.

Table 2.9 Stages in development of two models for measuring quality of life

Stage	Rolls-Royce Model	Volkswagen Model
Item selection	Literature review. Consultation (comprehensive) with health care workers. Use of existing instruments. Semistructured interview with 50 to 100 patients.	Use of existing instruments. Consultation with health care workers.
Reduction of no. of items	Use of second item-selection questionnaire identifying item frequency and importance. Choice of items with highest frequency-importance product or principal-component analysis.	Only items needed in item-selection process selected.
Questionnaire format	Choice of response-options scale: 7- to 10-point Likert or visual analogue scale. Time specification. Availability of previous responses to patients.	As for Rolls-Royce model.
Pretesting	Use of about 20 subjects. Analysis of results to ensure that full range of response options is used.	Use of 2 or 3 subjects.
Sampling for above four stages	Use of random sample of patients eligible for subsequent trials to ensure representation of entire range of disease severity, age, lifestyle, etc.	Use of sample of convenience.
Reproducibility and responsiveness	Questionnaire administration to stable patients, duplicating conditions of subsequent trial(s). Administration before and after intervention of known efficacy.	No testing before trial(s).
Validity	Use of construct validity. Use of *a priori* predictions.	Use of face validity.

Source: Guyatt *et al.*, 1986.

Table 2.10 Disease specific measures

Measure	Reference
Arthritis	
McMaster-Toronto Arthritis Patient Preference Disability Questionnaire (MACTAR)	Tugwell et al. (1987)
Health Assessment Questionnaire (HAQ)	Fries et al. (1980)
Functional Capacity Questionnaire	Helewa et al. (1982)
American Rheumatism Association Classification	Steinbrocker et al. (1949)
Arthritis Impact Measurement Scales (AIMS)	Meenan et al. (1982)
AIMS 2	Meenan et al. (1992)
WOMAC	Bellamy et al. (1988)
Back Pain	
Disability Questionnaire	Roland and Morris (1983)
Waddell Disability Index	Waddell and Main (1984)
Oswestry Low Back Pain Disability Questionnaire	Fairbank et al. (1980)
Cancer	
Instrument for Assessing QL	Selby et al. (1984)
Linear Analogue Self-Assessment (LASA)	Priestman and Baum (1976)
Vitagram	Nou and Aberg (1980)
Karnofsky Performance Status Index	Karnofsky and Burchenal (1949)
Spitzer (QOL) Index	Spitzer et al. (1981)
Functional Living Index: Cancer	Schipper et al. (1984)
Breast Cancer Questionnaire	Levine et al. (1988)
Rotterdam symptom check-list	de Haes et al. (1983)
EORTC quality of life questionnaire	Aaronson and Beckman (1987)
Chronic Lung Disease	
Dyspnoea Index	Mahler et al. (1984)
Chronic Respiratory Disease Questionnaire (CRDQ)	Guyatt et al. (1987)
Diabetes	
DCCT Questionnaire	DCCT Research Group (1987)
Digestive Diseases	
Rating Form of IBD Patient Concerns (RFIPC)	Drossman et al. (1989)
Inflammatory Bowel Disease Questionnaire (IBDQ)	Guyatt et al. (1989b)
Heart	
Specific Activity Scale (SAS)	Goldman et al. (1981)
Rose Chest Pain Questionnaire	Rose (1965)
New York Heart Association (NYHA) Functional Classification	Criteria Committee (1964)
Karolinska-Erasmus Classification	Olsson et al. (1986)

continued on page 38

Table 2.10 *continued*

Measure	Reference
Multiple Sclerosis	
Expanded Disability Status Scale (EDSS)	Kurtzke (1983)
Minimal Record of Disability	Slater *et al.* (1984)
Pain	
McGill Pain Questionnaire	Melzack (1975)
Visual Analogue Pain Rating Scales	Scott and Huskisson (1976)
ADL Pain Scale	Callahan *et al.* (1987)

A popular measure in arthritis assessment has been the Arthritis Impact Measurement Scale (AIMS) which was designed by Meenan and his colleagues (1980) in an attempt to provide a broader measure of the impact of arthritis on the patient's health than that indicated by the traditional measures of disease activity. Of interest is that the developers chose to adapt some of the elements of other instruments, namely the Katz Index of ADL, the Rand measures and the Quality of Well-Being Scale. The AIMS questionnaire contains 45 items grouped into 9 dimensions (see Figure 2.3). The dimension scores can be combined to produce overall models of health status, with 3 or 5 components. The questionnaire has been used by a number of investigators to study arthritis health status in a variety of settings, and has been translated into different languages (French, Spanish, and Dutch) (Meenan *et al.*, 1992).

The careful thought put into the development of this disease-specific instrument plus the willingness to develop and improve the measure, is reflected in the construction of a new, revised and expanded version, christened AIMS2. It is worth noting the reasons for the evolution of the measure (Meenan *et al.*, 1992).

> First we recognized that the items and scales in the AIMS1 could be improved by deleting weak items and by using a more consistent format for the remaining items. Second, we realized that there were arthritis-relevant aspects of health status that were not well addressed in the AIMS1. Finally, other investigators have raised concerns about approaches to arthritis health status assessment that were not part of the original AIMS approach.

The result of the researchers' endeavours produced new dimensions in arm function, work, and social support. In addition, satisfaction with function, attribution of problems to arthritis, and self-designation of priority areas for improvement were incorporated. These three areas clearly indicate a more direct concern for patient involvement. It also appears that the AIMS approach has become somewhat more generic!

Figure 2.3 AIMS questionnaire

Mobility
4 Are you in bed or chair for most or all of the day because of your health?
3 Are you able to use public transportation?
2 When you travel around your community, does someone have to assist you because of your health?
1 Do you have to stay indoors most or all of the day because of your health?

Physical Activity
5 Are you unable to walk unless you are assisted by another person or by a cane, crutches, artificial limbs, or braces?
4 Do you have any trouble either walking one block or climbing one flight of stairs because of your health?
3 Do you have any trouble either walking several blocks or climbing a few flights of stairs because of your health?
2 Do you have trouble bending, lifting, or stooping because of your health?
1 Does your health limit the kind of vigorous activities you can do such as running, lifting heavy objects, or participating in strenuous sports?

Dexterity
5 Can you easily write with a pen or pencil?
4 Can you easily turn a key in a lock?
3 Can you easily button articles of clothing?
2 Can you easily tie a pair of shoes?
1 Can you easily open a jar of food?

Social role
7 If you had to take medicine, could you take all your own medicine?
6 If you had a telephone, would you be able to use it?
5 Do you handle your own money?
4 If you had a kitchen, could you prepare your own meals?
3 If you had a laundry facilities (washer, dryer, etc.) could you do your own laundry?
2 If you had the necessary

Activities of Daily Living
4 How much help do you need to use the toilet?
3 How well are you able to move around?
2 How much help do you need in getting dressed?
1 When you bathe, either a sponge bath, tub or shower, how much help do you need?

Pain
4 During the past month, how often have you had severe pain from your arthritis?
3 During the past month, how would you describe the arthritis pain you usually have?
2 During the past month, how long has your morning stiffness usually lasted from the time you wake up?
1 During the past month, how often have you had pain in two or more joints at the same time?

Depression
6 During the past month, how often did you feel that others would be better off if you were dead?
5 How often during the past month have you felt so down in the dumps that nothing could cheer you up?
4 How much of the time during the past month have you felt downhearted and blue?
3 How often during the past month did you feel that nothing turned out for you the way you wanted it to?
2 During the past month, how much of the time have you been in low or very low spirits?
1 During the past month, how much of the time have you enjoyed the things you do?

Anxiety
6 During the past month, how much of the time have you felt tense or 'high strung'?
5 How much have you been bothered by nervousness, or your 'nerves' during the past month?
4 How often during the past month did you find yourself having

> transportation, could you go shopping for groceries or clothes?
> 1 If you had household tools and appliances (vacuum, mops, etc.), could you do your own housework?
>
> **Social Activity**
> 5 About how often were you on the telephone with close friends or relatives during the past month?
> 4 Has there been a change in the frequency or quality of your sexual relationships during the past month?
> 3 During the past month, about how often have you had friends or relatives to your home?
> 2 During the past month, about how often did you get together socially with friends or relatives?
> 1 During the past month, how often have you visited with friends or relatives at their homes?
>
> difficulty trying to calm down?
> 3 How much of the time during the past month were you able to relax without difficulty?
> 2 How much of the time during the past month have you felt calm and peaceful?
> 1 How much of the time during the past month did you feel relaxed and free of tension?
>
> The Arthritis Impact Measurement Scale (AIMS) questionnaire. Each group of items is listed in Guttman scale order with the scale levels in the left column. Subjects failing an item also tend to fail all lower items in the group.
>
> *Source*: Meenan *et al.*, 1980. Reproduced with the permission of J.B. Lippincott Company.

Another popular measure in arthritis assessment has been the Health Assessment Questionnaire (HAQ). The HAQ is a five-dimension measure: death, disability, discomfort, drug side-reactions, and economic impact (Fries *et al.*, 1980). It has also been adapted (Pincus *et al.*, 1983) to produce the Modified HAQ (MHAQ).

This measure is well within the tradition of functional assessment which has been adapted for a specific disease. The reason for mentioning another arthritis measure is that Fries, the prime mover in the development of the HAQ, has made some very strong claims to the effect that the components of the measure provide just as 'hard' (as opposed to 'soft') data on the outcomes of arthritis interventions as other more 'traditional' indicators, such as those generated by laboratory tests (Fries, 1983). This 'hard'/'soft' distinction is further investigated in the 'process/outcome' review (Ch. 4).

Mental Health Status

This area of measurement is worth attention for two main reasons:

1. The measurement of mental and psychiatric disorder is important for diagnostic and clinical management purposes: Granick (1983) has suggested that psychological assessment can be used in the following medical areas – psychiatric and neurologic disturbances, psychosomatic disorders, circulatory diseases (especially hypertension), diabetes, chronic pain, sexual dysfunctions, and gastrointestinal problems.

An Outline of the Development of Health Status Measures

2. Psychological health or 'subjective well-being' is an important component of the broader measurement of health status and quality of life. Perhaps it should be added that concern for mental health has taken on a greater importance in modern times as mortality has become less of a concern in medicine, as noted in Chapter 1, with the concomitant increase in the perceived significance of the quality of life. We have seen already that the generic measures all contain the mental functioning dimension.

McDowell and Newell (1987) point to the many attempts to distinguish between 'distress' and 'disorder', and between 'psychological', 'emotional', and 'mental' well-being. They argue that these attempts were not always successful and that the development of the field has been accompanied by disputes over the intent and conceptual interpretation of the various measures. In so far as mental functioning is a part of the wider approach to health status measurement it is clear that their concerns are of relevance in the present context. Wilkin *et al.* (1992) are, however, of the opinion that by contrast with the physical functioning and ADL measures there *has* been explicit conceptual analysis and careful validation of mental health.

McDowell and Newell think the General Health Questionnaire (GHQ) does have a clear conceptual focus. They suggest that this measure provides a good method for screening for general psychological and psychiatric disorder, thus proving useful for the matters listed by Granick (1983). The GHQ measure comes in several formats ranging from 60 to 12 items (Goldberg and Williams, 1988).

On subjective well-being McDowell and Newell suggest that the Bradburn (1969) Affect Balance Scale and to some extent the Dupuy (1984) General Well-being Schedule and GHQ measures address the notion of subjective well-being. Development in the field occurred with the incorporation of the mental dimension into the Rand measures of health status. This was termed the Mental Health Inventory (MHI): see Table 2.11 (Ware *et al.*, 1984). The Rand measures were shortened and simplified, so that the five-item mental health scale (MHI-5) was constructed from the 5 items that best predicted the summary score for the 38-item MHI. These 5 items are part of the SF-36 instrument (Ware and Sherbourne, 1992).

These developments in the mental functioning area demonstrate a not-untypical pattern of events in health status measurement. Starting from the narrower set of concerns about psychological disorder, subjective well-being was brought into the picture and incorporated into the generic measures. As with other generic measures, the Rand researchers felt their instrument to be somewhat unwieldy and so constructed 'reduced form' versions which provided what is claimed to be an equally valid approach to the measurement of, in this case, mental functioning.

Table 2.11 Sample items from the Mental Health Inventory (MHI)

Subscale	Number of items	Sample items
Anxiety	10	How much of the time during the past month have you been a very nervous person?
Depression	5	Did you feel depressed during the past month?
Loss of behavioural/emotional control	9	During the past month have you had any reason to wonder if you were losing your mind, or losing control over the way you act, talk, feel, or of your memory?
General positive affect	12	During the past month, how much of the time have you felt that the future looks hopeful and promising?
Emotional ties	2	During the past month, how much of the time have you felt loved and wanted?

Source: Ware et al., 1984.

Table 2.12 Mental instruments

Instrument	Reference
Mental Health Inventory (MHI)	Ware et al. (1984)
General Health Questionnaire (GHQ)	Goldberg (1978)
Affect Balance Scale	Bradburn (1969)
Profile and Mood States (POMS)	McNair et al. (1971)
Health Opinion Survey	Macmillan (1957)
22-Item Screening Score	Langner et al. (1963)
General Well-Being Schedule	Dupuy (1984)

As with all the measures we are considering, mental health measures should meet the appropriate methodological requirements such as reliability and validity, as discussed in the next chapter. A short list of mental instruments is presented in Table 2.12.

Utility Measures

The perils of adopting a particular classification of health status measures, such as the one used in this chapter, are brought out over the question of utility measures. Some analysts have argued strongly that the concept of utility can provide a unifying structure in which to place health status and quality-of-life measurement (Torrance, 1987; Feeny and Torrance, 1989). The common terminology then becomes that of the measurement of 'health state utilities'. Thus the Quality of Well-Being, the Rosser-Kind measure, and Torrance's own approaches could all be viewed as utility measures. Further, *any* measure employing the standard gamble scaling technique for health state valuations would be deemed to conform to the expected utility method of handling utility valuations in a risky world. Essentially it is the generic measures in their aggregate (index) form that are capable of sustaining this approach. In addition there have been other attempts to construct specific utility functions which are independent of these generic measures. Further, it should be noted that quality-adjusted life-years (QALYs), to be discussed in detail in Chapters 5 and 7, can be constructed using the generic measures described in the present chapter or they can be generated by finding the values of specified utility functions.

A good (and hopefully simple to comprehend) example of an 'independent' utility measure is that of Miyamoto and Eraker (1985). They constructed a utility function of the form $U(Y, Q) = bY^r H(Q)$, where Y is survival duration and Q is health status, r is a parameter reflecting the patient's risk attitude towards gambles involving survival duration and $H(Q)$ measures the utility of survival in health state Q, usually a state of less than full health; b is a scaling constant. The usefulness in describing this function is that it shows a method of focusing directly on the interactions between the risks attached to survival and the patient's health status. It also shows that, in principle at least, it ought to be possible to attach valuations, in utility form, to these inter-related considerations. Clearly it would then be necessary to 'get out into the field' and derive utilities in differing disease, condition, and health and medical intervention circumstances; or to develop utility-based QALYs of general application.

We return to the contemplation of risk in the health status context in Chapter 5, where the standard gamble method of scaling or evaluating health states is described.

This chapter has described various approaches to health status measurement. It can be argued that even this reasonably comprehensive picture is incomplete. A fuller description of measures could include what McDowell and Newell (1987) term *social health* measures − a glance at some of the names will indicate their scope: the Social Relationship Scale, the Social Maladjustment Schedule, the Interview Schedule for Social Interaction. It might also include a veritable battery of measures of *quality of life*. The relationships between health status measurement and quality of life measurement are further contemplated in Chapter 4. Some authors, including McDowell and Newell, would opt to describe a number of *pain measurements*. Further, there is a substantial literature on *patient satisfaction*. Simply mentioning these other measures indicates the huge scope of the developments in the measurement of health activities. Whilst admitting this scope and ever-mindful of 'holistic' concerns, we shall concentrate largely on the issues surrounding the construction and development of the narrower set of measures outlined in this chapter.

CHAPTER 3
Methodology

'Methodology' is a term we shall use to cover a number of concepts for consideration in this chapter. Treatment of methodological issues is not without controversy. Many analysts have been insistent that strict procedures be adopted in the construction and use of health status measures, that such measures thus meet exacting methodological standards. Others recoil from such formality – if outcome measures in health achieve their purposes in allowing judgements to be made about the usefulness or otherwise of health interventions then perhaps methodological issues need not be addressed too closely. Indeed, the argument goes, too much formality might destroy what 'art' there is in medical and health practices. O'Brien's (1989) comment is apposite: 'In interpreting clinical studies we need reasonable knowledge of disease and how it is measured and being overly impressed by power analyses and statistical theory may obscure important clinical results.' Judging, however, from the number of attempts by various authors in medical journals in recent years to try to persuade researchers and practitioners to conduct and to report upon their studies according to 'sound' scientific and methodological procedures, one would be bound to say that the attention paid to methodological issues has assumed greater significance lately. This applies right across the board of medical endeavour, not just health status measurement.

Confirmation of this trend is the publication of a textbook (Streiner and Norman, 1989) devoted explicitly to measurement in health, in particular what they term 'subjective states'. They point out that a sound methodology has been developed in psychology and education but that, not surprisingly, the available texts concentrate on these disciplines and thus focus on achievement, intelligence and personality tests. Recognition that 'psychometric' approaches could appropriately (perhaps even *should*) be used in health status measurement occurred some time ago, but formal texts have been lacking. Streiner and Norman present the methodology in a concise and very accessible manner and we make use below of their explanation of the basic reliability concepts.

It has become evident that many of the empirical studies undertaken in health status measurement in recent years now almost routinely pay attention to methodological criteria, possibly as one result of the aforementioned published advice! For example, around three-quarters of the relevant references in a major bibliography address reliability and validity criteria (Spilker *et al.*, 1990). Another relevant trend is that although new health status measures continue to be developed (a count in the Spilker bibliography showed 66 new instruments published since 1985), many more explorations and applications of existing measures are being published. This may be something to do with the judgement that these measures are reliable and well-validated. This judgement may not be justified for all the measures and claims for reliability and validity should always be scrutinised. Of course the new studies may well be adding to the body of evidence on these matters. A variation on this trend is the increasing tendency to adapt existing measures for the purposes at hand rather than develop new measures. Care must be taken in such cases that the adaptations do not give new measures which are unreliable or invalid. What criteria, then, are required for 'sound' health status measurement? Ideally we would like a health measure to be relevant to the question being studied or the problem to be resolved, to be capable of operational definition, to be credible in terms of its comprehensibility and acceptance to clinicians and other decision-makers, to be accurate, reliable and valid. At the same time these criteria should be met at 'reasonable' cost! Achievement of these tasks also raises of course the question of data availability and retrievability. These criteria are not by any means mutually exclusive. Thus, for example, operational definition is likely to be related to validity, credibility to reliability, and so forth.

We will focus upon five matters; (i) accuracy and reliability, (ii) validity, (iii) responsiveness, (iv) generalisability, (v) sensibility, and (vi) practicality.

ACCURACY AND RELIABILITY

Many aspects of these criteria will be familiar to readers exposed to statistical training. Use is made here of the excellent explanation furnished in an article by Chambers (1983), and of Streiner and Norman (1989).

A measure is deemed to be accurate if it reflects the 'true' state of the attribute being measured.

Measured Value = True Value + Systematic Error + Random Error

The usefulness of measurement depends on the extent to which the true value is obscured by the two types of error. Random error (sometimes termed 'noise') occurs when repeated measurements of some variable do not give the same values but there is no systematic deviation from the true value. Systematic error (bias) occurs when measurements deviate systematically (non-randomly) from the true value.

Why do these errors occur? Firstly, sampling error – this can result from problems of definition of the population or sampling frame or in the enumeration of non-response problems. Such error would usually constitute systematic error. Second, measurement error: this is where issues of reliability arise. Within (intra-)observer error can occur for repeated measures by the same observer: usually this is unsystematic error. Between (inter-) observer error may occur for measures by different observers; this is usually systematic. Within subject (respondent) error can also happen: this can be either systematic or unsystematic. Finally, error can result from the measurement instrument itself; poorly worded questions, for example.

Let us expand on the concept of reliability. For an instrument to be reliable 'measurements of individuals on different occasions, or by different observers, or by similar or parallel tests', should 'produce the same or similar results' (Streiner and Norman, 1989). The difficulty is that we are dealing with subjective scales and each scale produces a different measure from every other scale. 'To circumvent this problem, reliability is usually quoted as a ratio of the variability between individuals to the total variability in the scores.' Thus 'reliability is a measure of the proportion of the variability in scores which was due to true differences between individuals'. Hence reliability scores range between 0 (no reliability) and 1 (perfect reliability).

Two key matters are addressed in reliability testing: internal consistency and stability. *Internal consistency* calculations are based on a *single* administration of the measure being used and represent the average of the correlations among all the items in the measure. The scoring of individual items within a measure ought to be highly correlated if the measure is to be reliable. Various statistical techniques are available for these calculations. Since, however, there is only a single administration of the measure no account is taken of day-to-day variation or inter-observer variation, leading to 'an optimistic interpretation of the true reliability of the test' (Streiner and Norman, 1989).

Tests of *stability* concern the reproducibility of a measure administered on different occasions. In particular the following can be checked: inter-observer reliability – the degree of agreement between different observers: intra-observer reliability – the agreement between observations made by the same observer on separate occasions; and test–retest reliability – observations (on a patient, say) on two occasions separated by some time interval.

The question arises as to what should be regarded as acceptable reliability: how is a reliability coefficient score of between 0 and 1 to be interpreted? And what score gives the minimum acceptable level of reliability? The answer varies among analysts – Streiner and Norman suggest 0.85 for internal consistency and 0.5 for stability.

Internal consistency has been extensively reported for many of the measures referred to in Chapter 2: the texts by McDowell and Newell (1987) and by Bowling (1991) contain substantive detail. To give a recent example, the SF-36 was used in a postal questionnaire of 1980 patients in Sheffield (Brazier et al., 1992). For the 1582 respondents the Cronbach's α test exceeded the recommended minimum of 0.85 on all the dimensions of the instrument. Test–retest results were also acceptable.

For advice on the actual procedures to be followed in meeting reliability criteria we can turn to the guidelines of the American Psychological Association (1974). These guidelines cover as many as 19 recommendations plus 6 further 'characteristics' and deal also with validity (see below). We will confine ourselves to those of most importance in health status measurement.

When reporting a health status measure its reliability should be presented along with estimates of the standard error of measurement. How reliability was determined should be stated. If the measure has been used or standardised with more than one group or type of population sample, results of reliability studies should be given for each group. Stability of measurement scores over time should be studied, if feasible, by repeated administration of the same or a parallel form of the measurement instrument used. Variations in results should be reported, along with possible explanations. Further, analysis of internal consistency should be carried through and reported.

Finally, one group of authors (Ware *et al.*, 1981) have suggested a number of 'rules of thumb' concerning reliability:

1. Poorer reliability can be expected from short scales, a health status measure with few items would fall into this category.
2. Higher reliability coefficients cost more than lower ones, since they require more information – items or observers or both – so a trade-off between reliability and cost may be required.
3. Reliability tends to be lower for disadvantaged persons (especially in respect of income and education).

Thus, whilst it is important to ensure that health status measurement is conducted in a reliable manner, there may well arise some dilemmas concerning the degree of reliability required in relation to other salient features such as cost.

VALIDITY

We turn now to a key aspect of methodology which has perhaps not received the level of attention it deserves in health status measurement, although the situation is changing. This concept is concerned with the 'meaningfulness' of a health status measure. A valid 'score' on any such measure clearly should contain information about health status and not some other variable. Validity is a multi-faceted concept. We shall briefly consider the different types of validity but it must be stressed that the treatment is not comprehensive: the aim is simply to give an insight into this aspect of methodology. We make use of the guidelines for the methodological evaluation of functional assessment measures suggested by Bombardier and Tugwell (1987): see figure 3.1.

Face Validity

This refers to whether the method of aggregating individual items into a health status measure appears sensible. We are literally concerned with whether we are willing to accept the measure at 'face value' or not. Clearly, if we are not, then we need proceed no further – we are unconvinced about the validity of the measure. There are problems here, however, with the apparently subjective nature of the judgement to be made and with the inability to test statistically for this sort of validity.

It will be noted from Figure 3.1 that Bombardier and Tugwell (1987) use the term *credibility* in suggesting a series of questions by which to judge the face validity of a measure. Observe from the figure that they are concerned with whether items are measured in a 'sensible' way and whether a potential user judges that the measure is appropriate for his or her own purpose.

Content Validity

Face and content validity are closely related, so handling both types of validity simultaneously may help overcome the problems with face validity noted above. For content validity a measure is validated with respect to the choice of, and the relative importance given to, each item of the measure in relation to the purpose of the measure. In this respect we should note that various indices may have different uses and may be used at different levels of medical decision-making: thus there are diagnostic, prognostic, and therapeutic indices. In our context of health status measurement we seek to validate measures which will enable outcomes to be judged. These indices and measures can be intrinsically different – an index or measure developed for one of the purposes just outlined may not be appropriate for another. Thus the essential prerequisite for content validity is to be clear as to the purpose of the measure that has been developed. It can be seen from Figure 3.1 that Bombardier and Tugwell ask at the outset what the purpose of the health measure is. In judging content validity they use the term *comprehensiveness* and ask whether all the relevant dimensions are included and whether the method for selecting items for inclusion was appropriate.

Figure 3.1 Functional assessments: guidelines for evaluation

                                                                                  YES/NO

DISABILITY ASSESSMENT: _____
PURPOSE:
1) Is the purpose of the instrument clearly stated? .... ☐ ☐
      ___ Description   ___ Prediction   ___ Evaluation
COMPREHENSIVENESS (Content Validity)
2) Are all relevant dimensions of function included? .... ☐ ☐
      ___ Self Care   ___ Social Interactions
      ___ Mobility/Physical Activity   ___ Leisure Activities
      ___ Role Activities   ___ Emotional/Mental Function
      ___ Communication   ___ Other
3) Was the method of selecting items for inclusion appropriate? .... ☐ ☐
      ___ Investigator(s)/Clinicians(s) judgement
      ___ Patient(s) judgement
      ___ Group Consensus Techniques (Specify _____)
      ___ Statistical Technique of Data Reduction
            (Specify _____)
CREDIBILITY (Face Validity)
4) Are the items measured in a sensible way? .... ☐ ☐
   a) How specific are the questions?
          ___ dimension (ie. physical function)
          ___ subdimension (ie. self care, mobility)
          ___ component (ie. dressing, bathing)
          ___ behavioral activities (ie. tying shoes, buttoning shirt)
   b) Does each question refer to a specific time period?
      Specify _____
   c) What are the type and number of response categories for each question?
      Type of Scale: ___ difficulty   ___ dependence
                             ___ pain   ___ frequency
      Number of Response Categories:
      Specify _____
   d) Do the questions ask about:
      Function ___ or Change in Function ___
   e) Are the questions capacity or performance oriented?
      ___ Capacity mode ('Can you', 'Could you', 'Are you able to'?)
      ___ Performance mode ('Did you' ......?)
   f) Are the responses to individual questions aggregated to a summary score?
      ___ Yes   ___ No Specify method _____
5) Was this functional assessment developed and pretested for the
   purpose for which you want to use it .... ☐ ☐
ACCURACY (Criterion Validity)
6) Are the results reproducible? .... ☐ ☐
7) Does this functional assessment perform satisfactorily
   when compared to more accurate assessments? .... ☐ ☐
SENSITIVITY TO CHANGE (Discriminant Validity)
8) Is it sensitive enough to detect clinically important changes? .... ☐ ☐
      ___ across patients   ___ within patients
BIOLOGICAL SENSE (Construct Validity)
9) Does this assessment perform satisfactorily when compared
   to other similar assessments? .... ☐ ☐
FEASIBILITY
10) Is the format for administration appropriate for your purpose? .... ☐ ☐
      ___ Self administered
      ___ Interviewer administered
            ___ telephone   ___ records patients' answer
            ___ person to person   ___ records observation of
                                                               patients' performance
11) Is the time required to administer the questionnaire appropriate
    for your purpose? .... ☐ ☐
    Specify time _____
12) Are the questions easy to understand and acceptable to the
    patients and to the interviewer? .... ☐ ☐
                                                TOTAL POSITIVE ANSWERS _____

Source: Bombardier and Tugwell, 1987.

Criterion Validity

This type of validity concerns whether a measure produces consistent results which reflect the true state of the entity under scrutiny. This might concern, for example, the true clinical state of a patient, or the true health state of a member of some sample of persons under study. It is possible to divide criterion validity into two aspects: (*i*) predictive validity – where the time interval involved is a significant element in determining whether intervening experiences may affect expected or predicted results: (*ii*) concurrent validity – which relates to results on the criterion only at a specific point in time.

For criterion validity Bombardier and Tugwell are looking for accuracy: are the results on a measure reproducible and does the functional assessment measure compare well with other (known) accurate assessments?

Construct Validity

Also termed convergent validity, this type of validity is viewed by many analysts as a, or perhaps *the*, crucial test of the validity of an index or measure. A measure is validated with respect to its relationship to a theoretical idea or construct or concept that the measure's developer is trying to investigate. Validity thus depends on the consistency between the experimental measure (the health status measure) and one or more similar or related measures (not necessarily or even desirably other health status measures as such).

There is much talk in this context of 'Gold Standards' as the basic or ultimate test(s) of construct validity. And much disputation concerning what Gold Standard should be applied in each area of medical endeavour! To give an example: in measuring functional status we would presumably expect or predict that a sensitive and valid test of functional status would show lower (where lower means 'worse', functionally) scores in the elderly, in those with chronic disability conditions and in those unable to live their normal lives. Now clearly there may be available one or more tests of what constitutes disability. But lying behind the actual measurement of disability must be some (theoretical) notion which produces a set of criteria for judging the concept of disability. Perhaps this would involve inferring disability from the preferences or beliefs of both the disabled and anybody else, if asked, willing to make judgements on this concept.

This brief discussion harks back to the problem mentioned in the context of the functional assessment measures of the previous chapter: that disability is simply assumed as a concept in many assessment measures and not properly conceptualised. The point is that some 'outside' test, call it Gold Standard if you will, by which to judge the validity of the functional status measure under scrutiny is required. Perhaps we should give the last word on the matter to Bombardier and Tugwell (1987): 'Since there are no Gold Standards, construct validity implies a comparison of the instruments to be tested to other available instruments measuring similar concepts'.

Certainly there is plenty of evidence in the literature to show that this approach to construct validity is often used. The new DUKE profile, for example, has been tested for convergent validity against the Sickness Impact Profile, the Tennessee Self-Concept Scale and the Zung Self-Rating Depression Scale (Parkerson *et al.*, 1990). The study population included 683 primary care adult patients. The DUKE scores were compared with various socio-demographic characteristics, including age, gender, socioeconomic status and race.

Discriminant Validity

This type of validity is established if a series of unrelated and dissimilar measures yield different results from the experimental measure. This type of validity is really complementary to construct validity in the sense that we now require confirmation that our measure is to be discriminated from other measures: it is measuring something different and therefore should be distinguished. Testing for discriminant validity is thus a separate task from testing for construct validity.

A different usage may be noted in the context of clinical trials: here it has been used to refer to the ability of an index to distinguish clinically significant differences in therapeutic responses between patients and within patients. Note from Figure 3.1 that Bombardier and Tugwell refer to *sensitivity to change* and use the term 'clinically important changes'.

A number of studies combine convergent and discriminant validity to produce the test of *specificity*. Greenwald (1987) did this for the Sickness Impact Profile (SIP), the Profile of Mood States (POMS), and the McGill Pain Questionnaire (MPQ) in a sample of 536 persons with lung, pancreatic, prostatic, or cervical cancer. He suggests his findings generally support the specificity of these measures. He judges that the ability of the measures to distinguish ' conceptually different though often empirically related impacts of disease' is partial evidence of the general validity of these measures in surveys of the seriously ill.

This outline of the nature of validity indicates the complexity of the concept. It is, however, worth keeping in mind when contemplating the validity or otherwise of a health status measure the 'everyday' meaning or usage of the term 'valid'. We are in the habit of claiming that something is a valid way of looking at things or, perhaps more often, 'that's an invalid argument'. The criteria outlined above give an indication of what is involved in formally judging concepts of validity.

RESPONSIVENESS

This concept has been distinguished by some analysts from validity, whilst others treat it under discriminant validity. Wilkin *et al.* (1992) argue that 'the usually preferred methods of establishing validity and reliability tend to militate against responsiveness'. Guyatt (1988) states that responsiveness (or sensitivity to change) refers to a measure's ability to detect clinically important change. This is determined by two properties: first, a measure must yield more or less the same scores when subjects are stable, that is it should be reproducible. Second, it must register changes in score when the subject's health status changes. Various techniques are available for assessing responsiveness (Patrick and Deyo, 1989): the relative efficiency statistic (a ratio of paired t statistics), correlation of scale changes with other measures, receiver operating characteristic curves and a responsiveness statistic (ratio of minimal clinically important difference to variability in stable subjects).

Examples of attention to responsiveness are presented by Guyatt *et al.* (1989a) in the context of studies of breast cancer and inflammatory bowel disease. Meanwhile Wilkin *et al.* (1992) remark forcefully: 'In the review of instruments which follows in later chapters, we have been forced to remark far too often that there is an absence of evidence concerning responsiveness to change.' They do feel, however, that appropriate techniques are being developed which should enable better evidence on responsiveness to appear over the next few years. This is an interesting instance of change in the context of the methodological issues surrounding health status measurement.

GENERALISABILITY

This concept is simple and straightforward. It refers to questions of a measure's comparability across different diseases, conditions, populations and different types of investigations. Thus: will a questionnaire from an ambulatory setting be useful among inpatients? Will a valid questionnaire for young adults be equally valid in a geriatric population? Will an instrument that is valid and relevant for one cultural or clinical group be equally valid for others? Such questions of course are of most relevance for measures which purport to be general or generic. Generalisability in the disease-specific context could involve cross-cultural studies and/or translation (and adaptation) of measures into different languages (Patrick and Deyo, 1989).

SENSIBILITY

This concept is advocated by, for example, Feinstein and his co-authors (1986). Basically these writers are concerned that instrument developers do not get carried away in testing for statistical coefficients of quantitative reliability and validity but pay careful attention towards 'clinical sensibility'. This is achieved by first examining the specific purpose and clinical setting for which the measure will be used. If the measure is deemed appropriate on these characteristics then it will be sensible to use it. Second, the ease of use and of analysis of a measure should be addressed. If too much time and energy are needed to obtain the data, or if too much complexity is likely to be evident in analysing the results, the investigators might well be advised to choose another measure, or develop a simple new one, according to the authors.

PRACTICALITY

The notion of sensibility is clearly related to practicality. Thus it has already been hinted that costs may count! As health status measurement has burgeoned in recent years it is not surprising that potential users of health status measures, especially those operating in the clinical context, and decision-makers at different levels of resource allocation, have raised a series of questions about the usefulness of such measures. Many of the issues raised can be brought under the head of 'practicality', so we shall review some of these matters now.

A word first is in order on the environment(s) in which it is proposed to conduct health status measurement. It may be that someone or more likely some group of people or an organisation wishes actually to develop a new measure: then all we have been discussing concerning methodology is of relevance and much of the practical advice will also be germane. On the other hand researchers or medical decision-makers may simply wish to use existing measures. Here it is strongly advised that potential users seek confirmation of the reliability, validity and responsiveness of the measures they propose to use. Beyond this, certain practical issues in the use of the measures may then arise. Thus what is 'practical' will vary according to the environmental context.

Bearing these considerations in mind, the rather obvious point can be made that a good look should be taken at the total measurement resources available and a decision made on how much could be devoted or indeed if anything should be devoted to the measurement of health status. Second, having decided to proceed, it is necessary to establish priorities for allocating these resources to various health status concepts. These decisions will require to be taken in the light of answers to practical questions such as: if interviews are required or questionnaires are to be completed, should these be in person, by phone, or self-administered? In this context the Bombardier and Tugwell (1987) guideline questions on *feasibility* are clearly appropriate.

Care must be taken to respect 'respondent burden', indicators of which include refusal rates, missing responses, and administration time. There is some evidence that this burden is potentially high, for example psychological risks may be associated with questions about sensitive and embarrassing topics, where respondents may become distressed by the nature of the tasks required of them.

Potential burdens on medical staff should also be recognised. If nursing staff, for example, are asked to administer questionnaires, care should be taken that such demands do not place unacceptable burdens on their workloads. It may also be the case that medical and nursing personnel could object to the measurement approaches being employed. In this respect the experience of a team from Leiden in the Netherlands should sound a cautionary note (Mistiaen et al., 1992). After one week of data collection using the Duke University Center Health Profile (DUHP) on a research programme concerning nursing workload the use of the questionnaire was stopped. Both nursing personnel and medical outpatient staff thought some of the questions too personal, but, ironically, the patients did not think so, and an 80 per cent response rate was achieved during the week. We shall further review these issues in later chapters, but the concluding remark of Mistiaen and his colleagues is worth recording: 'In addition to finding many questions intrusive, the medical staff considered the DUHP-questionnaire irrelevant for measuring health status.' We are moving here beyond matters of practicality, and it is not intended to focus attention on the alleged shortcomings of one particular instrument, but health status measurers should clearly try to be aware of the concerns of those working directly with patients.

Other practical advice is that those developing and using health status measures should work with the least complicated instruments and methods possible (subject of course to reliability and validity!), to which might be added that long litanies of functional activities are not practical for most settings. It may also be the case that indices or measures requiring a minimum of professional guidance or observation would permit wider usage of health status measures. Next, health status measurement results should be presented in an understandable manner: in particular scores and score changes should be accompanied by interpretative commentary.

Finally, we should not ignore the economics of measurement! To reinforce the point made at the outset, a comparison of the costs and benefits of the measurement activity itself ought to be addressed: there is little point in expending resources on health status measurement if the marginal benefit in terms of the quantity and quality of outcome data does not exceed the cost of generating these data.

The material presented in this chapter is intended to show the sort of methodological criteria that have been advocated for application in health status and quality-of-life measurement. As indicated at the outset, all the measures that have been developed have been 'tested' against these criteria, albeit in varying degrees. Reliability has been more of a focus than validity, and responsiveness has not been tested sufficiently (Wilkin *et al.*, 1992). The question of how sensible, practical and capable of being generalised are particular instruments perhaps requires more subjective judgement: commentary on the application of the measures in particular contexts (including possible barriers to measurement) appears in later chapters (especially 6 and 7.)

Several texts are now available which aim to guide potential users of measures on the methodological 'soundness' of named measures (McDowell and Newell, 1987; Wilkin *et al.*, 1992; Bowling, 1991). A variety of articles surveying the field of health status and/or quality-of-life measurement have provided analysis, in some cases quite critical, of these methodological issues. Nevertheless, and this will be taken up again in the final chapter, there is a relative lack of published independent critiques of the available measures.

CHAPTER 4

Quality as an Issue

Quality, like beauty, may well lie in the eye of the beholder. What is meant by 'quality' in medicine? Does good quality medicine lie in the bedside manner or general approachability of the doctor, of the nurse and of other health personnel? Does it lie in the quality of the 'hotel' services provided by hospitals? Does it lie in the effectiveness of the medical techniques applied, and in that case what do we mean by 'effectiveness'? Does it mean the quicker someone is returned to his or her normal lifestyle the higher quality the medical intervention? Does it mean the more services provided for a given level of resources the 'better'? Does it lie in the patient's perception of the process he or she has undergone? This series of questions gives the flavour of the complexity which attends the definition and content of the notion of quality.

Perhaps it is misleading or too simple to write of 'the' notion for what should be interpreted as a multi-faceted concept. Let us look at some of these facets: how far health needs are met (which raises the question of what is meant by 'need'); the effectiveness of medical intervention; the efficiency of intervention; the proportion of people benefiting from intervention and the evaluation of these benefits; the proportion of people adversely affected by intervention and the evaluation of such adverse effects; patient satisfaction; health service professional satisfactions; equity – the distribution of health resources and the distribution of the benefits accruing from their use. This is by no means an exhaustive list: it does serve though to confirm the complexity of the issues with which we are faced in this chapter.

We must now embark on an effort to explore some of these matters. We shall look at the issues surrounding quality, its interpretation and its measurement. An attempt will be made to relate health status measurement to what has been termed 'quality of life' measurement. We will look at medical audit and quality assurance and see whether notions of 'value for money' have a qualitative dimension. Throughout, there will be a continuing attempt to integrate the theme of change with the developing debate on the issues raised by the contemplation of quality.

Health interventions do not of course solely take the form of medical care. In order to keep matters on a reasonably simple footing, however, we will stick for the present to the terms 'medical care' or 'health care' in our discussion of quality. Note then that we are contemplating the quality of medical care as such. The concept of 'quality of life' could logically be separated from quality of care but is often interwoven, as this chapter seeks to show.

A QUALITY FRAMEWORK

Let us start by focusing on three broad aspects of quality. These are: structure, process, and outcome. Donabedian (1988b) describes these as three approaches to the assessment of quality, or three avenues to a judgement on quality, a framework he first adopted in 1966 (Donabedian, 1966), and one that has proved popular with many analysts since then. He insists that these three concepts are not to be viewed as dimensions or attributes of quality itself.

Structure refers to the resources that are made available for medical care: in physical terms these are medical and other personnel, hospitals, clinics, and technology of all kinds. Structure also encompasses the ways in which resources are provided, including organisation and the differing aspects of finance. *Process* concerns the ways in which the structure is used in diagnosis and treatment, including the patient's own activities in seeking treatment and making use of this treatment. *Outcome* as a concept is straightforward in description, if not necessarily in measurement! Outcome measurement focuses on the results of the medical care process for the health status of individuals and populations as the consequences of using the structure of resources. Outcome measures have been summed up as: death, disease, disability, discomfort and dissatisfaction. This list focuses on the 'downside': *reductions* in these elements through medical interventions would of course constitute improved outcomes. Outcomes can also include improvements in the patient's knowledge and changes in the patient's health-related behaviour.

Quality, then, relates to whether adequate resources allow adequate diagnosis and treatment, which may in turn lead to favourable health outcomes. Clearly we need criteria by which to judge what is 'adequate' and what is 'favourable'.

A rather neat characterisation of the structure-process-outcome framework is provided by McGlynn *et al.* (1988) in the context of mental health services, although they choose to reverse Donabedian's ordering because they wish to focus initially on outcomes to see what is implied for process and structure (see Figure 4.1). This diagram shows that, although structure can be separated in a categorical sense in setting an analytical framework for the analysis of medical care, there is little point in distinguishing the resource base from process and outcome in discussing the 'quality' of structure. What is adequate in terms of resources must surely relate to the uses to which these resources are put. Nevertheless it is common for people to refer to 'well-trained' manpower or 'high-quality' technology or 'well-equipped' clinics, the implication presumably being that these concepts in some sense

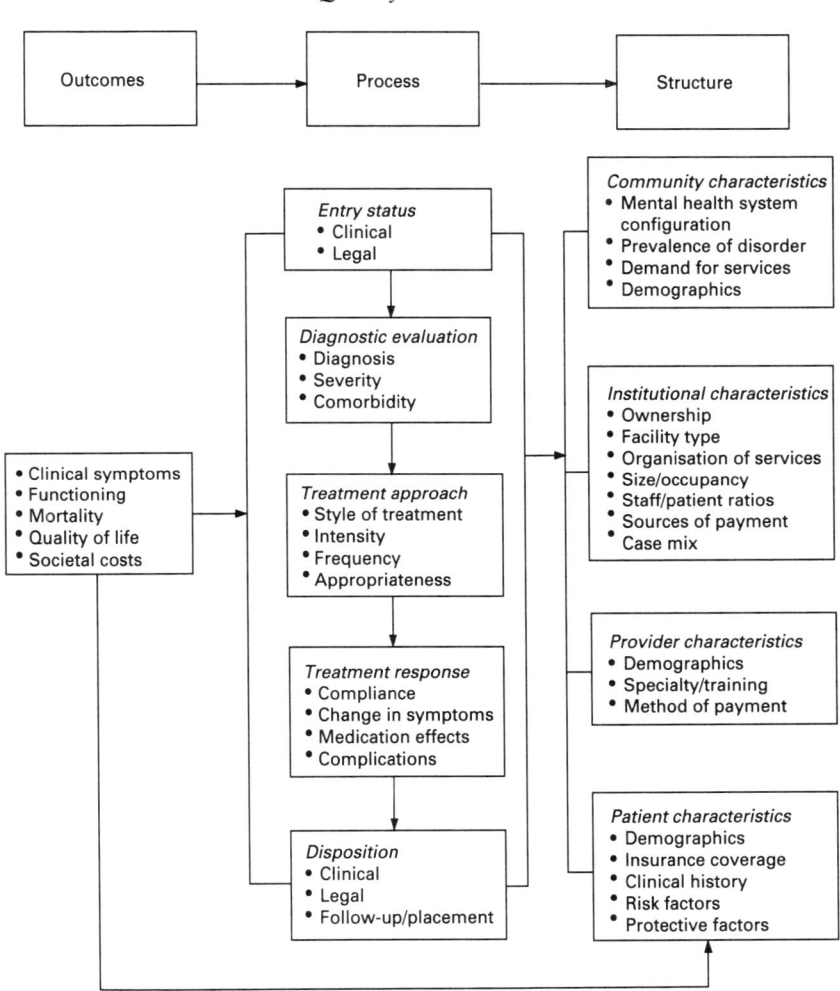

Figure 4.1 An analytic strategy for research on the quality of mental health services

Source: McGlynn et al. (1988).

have a status of their own, that they are to be valued for their own sake. This does not appear to take us very far: we really need to examine what use is made of these resources, that is to examine the processes of medical care and to trace through to the ultimate consequences for outcomes, of which five categories are listed in Figure 4.1, including quality of life.

Although Donabedian has expended much effort popularising this rather convenient framework for analysing quality he has been concerned to point to both antecedent and contemporaneous work which is in the same spirit. Modern analysts such as himself (Donabedian, 1989) have returned for inspiration to the life and work of Codman who was a tireless advocate for his 'end result' method in the United States in the early part of this century. The end result idea was that a hospital should follow the treatment of every patient long enough to determine whether this had been successful or not and, if not, why not. His system involved analysis of each patient's diagnosis, treatment, and results in the years subsequent to treatment. This allowed representative efficiency boards to redirect the policies, organisation, and operation of the hospital into more efficient channels. In reality he was monitoring outcome – specified as a 'satisfied or relieved patient' – and why the outcome may not have been favourable. He believed that his end result data would be useful in monitoring quality, advancing clinical science, establishing accountability, and allocating resources. All these would be recognised as key concerns by the practitioners of quality assurance in the present day.

Donabedian (1988b) also pays tribute to the 'ground-breaking' studies of maternal and perinatal mortality undertaken under the auspices of the New York Academy of Medicine in the early 1930s.

Another luminary, a contemporary of Donabedian's, has been Williamson. His *health accounting* idea is that quality assurance (QA) must integrate the health and management sciences to analyse health care benefits and disbenefits 'with the same rigor as is applied to the analysis of fiscal profits and losses' (Williamson, 1988). Again the emphasis is on outcomes with suggested priorities based on 'achievable benefits not achieved'. He suggests that quality assurance should be carried out on the basic premises that:

1. It is not whether but how well QA is conducted.
2. Problem-solving principles apply at individual, institutional, national and international levels of aggregation.
3. QA must be based on a foundation of integrated disciplines.

The concept of QA is given a further airing in the present chapter, but to bring the assessment of quality story up to date we can cite Donabedian's (1988b) suggestion that the tradition is continued in the indicators used as structure and process criteria by the Joint Commission for Accreditation of Health Care Organizations (JCAH) in the United States (Lehmann, 1987). Amongst other matters the JCAH's reviewers check for the existence of monitoring equipment in operating theatres, the adequacy of procedures to give hospital privileges to staff physicians, and whether there are active and well-attended hospital activities, such as surgical morbidity and mortality conferences to review untoward events. These could be regarded as review of structure. Process criteria include whether medical records are dictated and signed timeously, whether laboratory tests are used appropriately, and whether relevant parts of the physical examination are performed and recorded in the medical records.

PROCESS AND OUTCOME

It would be remiss not to discuss an important controversy which persists in discussions of the issue of quality in medical care, particularly as the inclusion of outcome measures in quality assessment has been gathering pace in recent years. This concerns the proposition that the issue be framed in terms of process *versus* outcome. At first sight this would appear to be a nondebate if we stick within the framework of structure-process-outcome suggested above: both process and outcome are essential components of an integrated framework. Undoubtedly, though, some interesting insights emerge if the components of the framework are analysed separately.

The resources must be there, as has been noted, but what relative significance should be attached to the process and outcome components? The answer to this question would presumably have some bearing or feedback on the resources required for 'good quality' medical care.

Bearing in mind that process is in large part concerned with the tools of diagnosis and treatment, what can be inferred from the results that are obtained on process measures? Consider diagnosis, clearly an art and clearly a process that can be qualitatively judged so that diagnostic skill can in principle be assessed. Now presumably a probability distribution of responses on diagnosis is possible, so that there may be no hard and fast 100 per cent sure response to the question: 'Is this really disease X?' It might also be pointed out that doctors have put enormous efforts into the task of describing particular diseases and their characteristics so that diseases can be recognised for what they are during the process of diagnosis. Now suppose we have an agreed set of criteria for diagnosis: how then can disease measurement be accomplished? One answer would be by the application of process measures. In arthritis, e.g., various tests can be conducted and measurements undertaken of the erythrocyte sedimentation rate (ESR), the level of antibody to DNA, and latex fixation titres. A comprehensive list of 'rheumatology standards' is shown in Table 4.1. Changes in these measurements for particular individuals may then be used to characterise changes in the course of arthritis for these individuals. It may then be stated that a person's disease condition has 'improved' – perhaps it is less 'active', as judged by the particular process measures on offer in relation to the criteria laid down for the measurement for disease activity in arthritis. This improvement may well have been brought about by a particular medical intervention, thus involving the second aspect of process: treatment. Hence good quality medicine might be judged by reference to process measurement of this sort.

Process measurement of the type just described undoubtedly has its attractions. The term 'hard' data can be used to describe data which are accurately determined, numeric, objective, and reproducible, in short data which permit quantitative assessment, not just qualitative. Many laboratory tests meet the sort of requirements outlined, although even here judgement may

Table 4.1 Rheumatology standards

1. Joint count
2. Patient-rated measure of pain relief
3. Global assessment of change in disease activity
4. Patient-rated measure of pain
5. Global assessment of disease activity
6. Duration of morning stiffness
7. Grip strength
8. Time to walk 50 feet
9. Joint swelling
10. ESR
11. Analgesic consumption
12. Time until onset of fatigue
13. Tenderness measured by instrument
14. Haemoglobin
15. Weight loss
16. Thermography
17. X-Ray
18. Rheumatoid factor
19. Technetium[99] uptake
20. Xenon[133] clearance

Source: Bombardier, Tugwell, Sinclair *et al.*, 1982.

be required. Stewart and Joyce (1988) suggest: 'Even simple observations such as the reading of an oscillating sphygmomanometer value frequently contain a judgmental element, and the more complex ones that come from the autopsy room or microbiology laboratory may depend heavily upon judgment.'

So wherein lies the process: outcome controversy? Partly, it could be argued, in the contention that these tests are the basic 'objective' tests of the nature of disease and its course in individuals. Such objective tests of process may also be intrinsically easier to measure, so that medical practitioners understand the results and feel able, perhaps because of their training, to interpret the data so generated. Thus 'soft' data, allegedly inferior since decidedly 'subjective', should at best take second place to hard data giving precise quantification to acts of process, it can be argued. Now there presumably are few doctors who believe that medical interventions should be judged solely on the grounds of laboratory or other process measurements, but it would be interesting to know how many doctors who are 'comfortable' with numeric results of the hard data variety in making judgements of a patient's progress or lack of it would also be sceptical of the allegedly 'softer' measures of outcome with which this book is largely concerned. One complication that should be addressed is that some measures are neither strictly process nor strictly outcome (but perhaps both)! Consider again Table 4.1 which lists what have been described as 'rheumatology standards'. Are 'grip strength' and 'time to walk 50 feet' process or outcome measures? Both, probably. But how far does this take us? How would medical judgements be made about a patient who had a 'slow' time but was doing 'well' on other criteria? Or what about the patient with a 'strong' grip but poor overall functioning?

Potential difficulties such as that just raised have led some observers to insist that health status measures, far from being 'soft', better meet the central characteristics that define 'hard' data – precision, quantification, reproducibility, inter-observer variation – than do laboratory and other process variables. In arthritis, to continue our example, disability assessment measures are claimed to be more reliable (Fries, 1983) as measurements of patient functioning than ESR, antibody level, or grip strength. An interesting development in the arthritis area is the use of arthritis and functional assessment measures (ADL, Modified Health Assessment Questionnaire and pain items) as aids in diagnosis! (Callahan and Pincus, 1990)

A problem in measuring quality using process indicators alone is that the relationship between the medical care process and health status is not always direct, perhaps being affected for example by patient compliance: adequate process may not result in good outcomes. Conversely, apparently poor process may lead to good outcomes because the process criteria selected are invalid or unreliable or even incorrectly measured. As has been pointed out (Schroeder, 1987), faced with a choice between good process with poor outcome and poor process with a good outcome, most patients and doctors would opt for the latter!

To show that we are not dealing here purely with a question of semantics we can cite an editorial in the *American Journal of Public Health* (1990) by Robert Kane. He would like to see the basis on which long-term nursing home care in the United States is funded moving from a process-driven approach to one based on outcomes. He suggests that nursing homes should be paid more if the observed improvement in a client is better than some suitable measure of expected improvement. This he thinks would free the nursing homes from the current regulatory and payments framework which he considers has provided little impetus for the homes to invest in the effort needed to help clients improve.

In fact new US regulations are enshrined in a law which took effect in October 1991. These concern Medicare and Medicaid participation, through the Health Care Financing Administration (HCFA), and since most nursing homes rely on these two systems for their financial survival, the importance of the reforms will be well recognised. Of particular interest in the present context is that a comprehensive functional assessment has to be undertaken immediately upon a person's admission to a facility. A stronger role is given/mandated to physicians and the focus is on quality of care and quality of life outcomes, although how much attention will actually be paid to outcomes in decisions concerning nursing home residents remains to be seen, so Kane's (1990) suggestion may not be fully acted upon. This example indicates that the resolution of the process: outcome dilemma could lead to significant shifts in resources use in this long-term care context (Wilensky, 1991).

One way round the alleged process: outcome dichotomy would be the suggestion that valid quality measurement lies not in the choice of elements of process or outcome but the relationship between the two components. Thus outcome quality may imply process quality – if this is the case then there is no dilemma. If not, as some empirical studies have shown, then process and outcome measures should be considered as independent but perhaps equally important measures of the quality of care. Thus if Kane is correct then it may be appropriate to use outcome measures in nursing care. This is perfectly acceptable, but the case clearly has to be made.

In summary we can come to a conclusion consistent with our original framework: namely, that process and outcome are both likely to be necessary in the assessment of quality, but that the circumstances will dictate the relative importance devoted to each. It is not necessary therefore to 'take sides' in some generalised sense. If this is the case then both components will provide feedback effects to the level and the nature of the resources that may or may not be provided for medical care. It is thus interesting to note that the JCAH (mentioned above) decided to explore the use of outcome criteria as part of its accreditation procedures, in addition to the structure and process criteria already employed.

It seems appropriate to give the last words on this matter to Donabedian, who is firmly of the view that elements of structure, process and outcome should be included in any system of assessment. In recent writings (Donabedian, 1988a,b) he has also been adamant that information about patient satisfaction should be indispensable to assessments of quality and to the design and management of health care systems. This element has been little used in assessing the quality of medical care, he claims, and furthermore: 'we know next to nothing about how professional judgments on quality of care would compare with the judgments of patients who received that care' (Donabedian, 1988b) . We can observe here a move towards the treatment of patient satisfaction measures as significant for quality assessment, a trend that will be further remarked upon in Chapter 7. The question of whose values to use in health assessment is treated in more detail in the next chapter.

MEDICAL AUDIT

We turn now to concepts/procedures which are related to or have a bearing on quality in medical care. Amongst all the controversies raging over the British Government's reforms first outlined in the *Working for Patients* White Paper (Department of Health, 1989a) few commentators appeared to be against the principle of medical audit. Now of course this concept was not invented at the time of the Government's NHS review in 1988. Murley (1989) recalls sitting in at a surgical death and morbidity meeting on Sir James Learmonth's unit in Edinburgh in 1948. Indications, however, of the current interest in the UK in this concept and its implications are: the inauguration in 1991 of a bimonthly newsletter entitled *Medical Audit News*, a special section of the *British Medical Journal* devoted to medical audit, and the increasing number of published studies appearing in the medical literature.

As good a definition as any of medical audit is that of the British Government: 'the systematic, critical analysis of the quality of medical care, including the procedures used for diagnosis and treatment, the use of resources, and the resulting outcome and quality of life for the patient' (Department of Health, 1989b). This encompasses all the themes we have been focusing upon in this chapter, if not the whole book!

The British Government is in favour of a largely profession-led framework for medical audit, building upon a number of professional initiatives, but with managerial input: this would be 'independent' audit, which 'may take the form of external peer review or a joint professional and managerial appraisal of a particular service'. Management, it is made clear, has significant responsibility for ensuring that resources are used in the most effective way. Now clearly the government has in mind the systematic review of the structure and process of medical care but is also in favour of developing a 'comprehensive set of measures of the outcome of much of the work of individual services and doctors' (Department of Health, 1989b).

This desire for outcome measures should come as no surprise to the readers of this book, given the general thrust of the themes we have been developing. However, it is interesting to observe the changing measurement environment, with two quite different health care systems, namely those of the United States and of the United Kingdom, converging on the view that outcome measurement should play a greater role in quality assessment.

Medical audit is faced with some formidable difficulties. Consider the development of indicators of comparative mortality rates across hospitals or other health institutions. (Florence Nightingale, it may be noted, was keen on this sort of data!) Death is probably the easiest outcome to agree about and detect, but one of the problems with using it as an outcome measure is that an important predictor of death is the severity of disease. Thus a study of paediatric intensive care units in nine teaching hospitals in the USA showed a sixfold difference in mortality rates, but when these rates were adjusted for differences in the initial severity of illness the mortality differences disappeared (Pollack *et al.*, 1987). Clearly the utmost care has to be used in studying comparative mortality rates since, e.g., hospitals handling the sickest patients might well register the worst outcomes.

Other factors for which control in evaluation may be called are diagnosis, indications for treatment, and physiological characteristics. Another problem that also has to be addressed is that important complications may not occur in patients until after discharge – how then to incorporate delayed mortality, or the possibility that someone may subsequently die in a health unit other than the unit where, say, a surgical operation took place?

It should be apparent that the considerations raised here apply equally strongly for outcome measures other than death. Indeed since medical audit evidently encompasses process as well as outcome, careful study will be required of the 'confounding' factors which attend the collection, collation and evaluation of comparative data for the purposes of audit.

QUALITY ASSURANCE

Quality Assurance (QA)

> denotes a spectrum of desirable characteristics of care: effectiveness, efficacy, efficiency, equity, acceptability, accessibility, adequacy, and scientific/technical quality. These can be measured by the consequences (for) health care: reduction of death, disease, disability, and complications and aggravations of disease; the enhancement, maintenance and restoration of health; the ability of treated patients to participate in economic and social life; the alleviation of pain and discomfort; humane conditions of death in terminal illness; general well-being; satisfaction of patients and consumers with care; and reasonable costs. (Johansen, 1989)

This astonishing litany is comprehensive, to say the least! The basic aims of QA are rather simpler to list, i.e. to improve health care in terms of outcome, functional ability, patient well-being, consumer satisfaction and the use of resources by shaping health policy and practice. The latter phrase is significant: medical audit and quality assurance must surely be linked with the potential for changing the way things are done and the way resources are or might be used.

The concept of technology assessment (TA) has been closely linked with QA. Banta and Andreasen (1990) regard TA as a comprehensive form of policy research which examines the short-term and long-term consequences of the application of technology. A comprehensive TA would encompass societal, economic, ethical, and legal issues. A significant amount of TA/QA work and research is being undertaken throughout Europe and North America, for example, in some cases with the active involvement of WHO. It is interesting to observe (Johansen, 1989) the variety of activities covered: communication technologies (information systems, use of computers), hospital infection control, variations in health care practices, TA for medical equipment (international insulin pump study across nine countries), use of laboratory procedures, drug use, imaging technologies (e.g. basic radiological system, magnetic resonance imaging). Much of this work is being accomplished on a collaborative and comparative basis across countries. It is worth stressing that this emphasis on TA/QA has been of recent provenance, being initiated in the European region of WHO in 1980, for example. In the United States the Office of Technology Assessment began a programme of technology assessments in 1975 and has by now assessed around 100 technologies.

QUALITY OF LIFE

One rather odd feature of the outpourings on quality of life has been the parallel literature which has developed with articles labelled 'quality of life' running along one line and others concerned with 'health status measurement' running along the other. This is odd because if the respective literatures are compared it is apparent that many of the dimensions and items incorporated into the quality of life indices are also used in the health status work, and yet little cross-referencing between the two bodies of work seems to occur. Is there something fundamental going on here or does it simply come down to a matter of labelling which could easily be sorted out with appropriate translation? This issue is worthy of brief consideration since we are concerned to explain the changing world of health status measurement and this particular pattern of development needs further elucidation.

But first let us examine the possible interpretations that can be placed on the term 'quality of life'. In an excellent article in which the authors are explicit about the ideological bases upon which quality of life might be judged, Edlund and Tancredi (1985) provide a useful taxonomy of the meanings of quality of life, a taxonomy which they also relate to policy choices, which will be considered in Chapters 6 and 7. The first meaning is quality of life as the fulfilment of personal goals. This meaning is of course subject to many interpretations, but no less distinguishable as a concept for that. A similar but not identical meaning is the individualistic view: quality of life is what each individual defines it to be. One problem with this interpretation is that individual values may conflict with social values, a conflict at its starkest, as Edlund and Tancredi point out, over the issue of suicide. Individuals may conclude that life is not worth living but society will often try to stop people exercising this option. However, it should be pointed out that suicide might be viewed as a social phenomenon in the sense that rates and trends vary markedly between countries.

A third meaning for quality of life is the ability to lead a 'normal life'. Unfortunately this innocuous-sounding term is essentially incapable of definition: each of us is likely to give our own interpretation of what constitutes 'normal'. A fourth possibility is the notion of quality of life as the ability to lead a 'socially useful life'. Again, this is capable of a multiplicity of interpretations, but let us focus briefly on this particular meaning. Our two authors make the important point that socially useful behaviour depends very strongly on the socio-political environment. To some policy-makers such behaviour may involve its citizens being gainfully employed and contributing to the national economy. This is clearly not acceptable when considering the quality of life of children, retired persons and the chronically ill. Retired persons, for example, frequently perform all sorts of 'socially useful' roles, not least in the family context. The key to understanding 'social utility' is to expose the criteria which are being used in given circumstances when quality of life is at issue, thus allowing assessment of policies which are being pursued in the name of social utility.

Another meaning of the quality of life revolves around the concepts of 'rational man'. Here the attempt is made to depart from the subjective – a term which can evidently be attached to the four previous meanings. 'Objective' truth is sought: rational persons, standing back from personal feelings and considerations, calmly weigh the evidence and pronounce on the appropriate course of action or, in the present context, the impact on the quality of life. This is not as fanciful as it sounds, calling in to play as it may the objective expert, a not unknown personage in health evaluation and health policy! A caricature of such a person would be someone placing excessive or indeed sole reliance on mathematical and numerical techniques. The trouble is that some technical experts may indeed come to believe that they are being impartial and objective in their judgements, thus obscuring to themselves and others the underlying assumptions and value judgements they are making. This little discussion could easily be related to the 'hard'/'soft' terminology used earlier in this chapter, with many of the process measures taking on the 'objective' tag. It is however clear that one should also look with a wary eye at the quantitative outcome measures, whether termed quality of life or health status measures, whose progenitors proclaim are entirely objective. The criterion of clinical sensibility put forward in Chapter 3 should also be borne in mind.

Let us now return to the issue raised at the start of this section and look more closely at the relationship between health status measurement and quality of life measurement. To do so we can use the excellent treatment by Bergner (1989). She argues initially that quality of life is not defined in published reports of clinical trials, so that it is necessary to deduce its meaning from the dimensions assessed and reported. These dimensions include physical, social and leisure activities, work, symptoms, loss of income, cognition, emotional adaptation, self-esteem, anxiety, stress, sexual activity, interpersonal relationships, impotence, incontinence, and overall satisfaction with life. It is clear from this list that if quality of life measures contain some or all of these dimensions then there is considerable overlap with what we have been terming health status measurement. Bergner also points out that some analysts are in favour of including environmental quality and the quality of community life as relevant outcomes, especially where health promotion activities are concerned. It may also be relevant to view quality of life as a risk factor or cause of illness as well as an outcome. Thus a stressful life may lead to an increased risk of heart disease, or environmental pollution may have adverse consequences on health. In this context the development of the mental health status measures (see Chapter 2) may have some relevance.

Are we now in danger of trying to deal with everything at once? If the focus is on health interventions should we not be trying to concentrate our analysis and evaluation on health-related entities? One answer would be to deal with what might be termed 'health-related quality of life', a phrase appearing with more regularity in the literature (Fitzpatrick, 1993; Fletcher, 1993). Thus it would be necessary to select for study and incorporation into health status measures those dimensions deemed relevant to the concept of health-related quality of life.

Bergner (1989) is more forthright. She believes there are striking differences between health status measurement and quality-of-life measurement as presently developed, especially in the level of conceptualisation: quality of life as used in clinical research is a vague term without conceptual clarity. By contrast, conceptual frameworks for health status 'have appeared in the literature, have been discussed and debated and have provided the underpinning of several measures'. This may be overdoing matters: sociologists, for example, may not be entirely happy with her view that there is inadequate conceptualisation in their attempts to capture the quality of life, attempts which have paid some attention to the relevant health dimensions. It should be stressed that Bergner is writing very much in the clinical evaluation context. For her, the dimensions of health status comprise the following: genetic foundation; biologic, physiologic, anatomic condition (disease/disability/handicap state); functional condition (performance: social/physical/cognitive); mental condition; and health potential.

In conclusion this analysis would appear to indicate that health status index developers need to pay careful attention to the conceptualisation and definition of health status in assessing both the quality of health interventions and the ensuing consequences for the quality of life.

QUALITY ASSESSMENT AS RESEARCH

In order to provide a unifying 'thread' and as a useful link with the discussion in Chapter 6 of the influence of health status measurement on decision-making it is worth taking on Berwick's suggestion that most if not all the work on quality assessment has been in the nature of research (Berwick, 1988). Writing in 1986/87, he claims that there is no applied 'technology' to study the quality of heath care, so that: 'despite its breadth and accomplishments, the academic activity has remained remarkably disconnected from the day-to-day workings of the industry it purports to study'. We shall return to this issue in Chapter 6 but use will be made at this juncture of Berwick's categorisation of the research.

He suggests that research on quality has had two main divisions. One line of research tries to define the targets of measurement, which are our old friends; structure, process and outcome. This line has been examined in some detail in the present chapter, of course. The second line of research deals with measurement methods through which to assess particular structures, processes, or outcomes. These methods can be classified as implicit, explicit, and sentinel. The implicit method uses expert opinion – acknowledged experts, peer groups – to make quality judgements, but without formal, explicit rules laid down in advance of the review procedure. Not surprisingly, the call may go up during such reviews for explicit guidelines. Explicit methods may proceed via expert panels developing prescriptive approaches (which could be quite formal – Berwick refers to 'algorithms') for the diagnosis and perhaps the care of a given disease. Once explicit rules are in place it may be possible for non-physicians, suitably trained, to review care and assign scores to reflect the degree of compliance with the explicit laid-down standards. This involvement of non-medics is not as surprising as it may appear: explicit review processes are used by regulatory bodies or quality assessment programmes independent of the physicians being reviewed. Chapter 6 goes into some detail concerning the changing relationships between implicit and explicit assessment of clinical decision-making practices.

Sentinel methods concern procedures or studies which look for unusual or 'outlying' events and values. This approach covers, for example, 'morbidity and mortality conferences' in surgery departments, and studies of variation in the use of health care resources – a matter briefly considered above in the discussion of medical audit.

To repeat, Berwick considers that most of the procedures outlined constitute study and research and the links between this work and everyday medical decision-making are somewhat tenuous. If he is right, then the 'quality researchers' have a major task in 'selling' their ideas and methods to health and medical decision-makers. There is perhaps some evidence that this is now happening: the areas in which health status measurement are increasingly being applied are examined in Chapter 7. In Chapter 6 we will take a further look at Berwick's reasons for his claim over the lack of applied health measurement technology.

This has been a fairly selective discussion of the issues surrounding quality, both of medical care and of life. The next chapter will look more closely at the measurement process in health status measurement and then Chapter 6 will, amongst other things, pick up some of the themes raised in the present chapter in the decision-making context.

CHAPTER 5

The Measurement Process

It was pointed out in Chapter 2 that in developing a health status measure essentially three steps are required:

1. The choice of dimensions/items/descriptors for inclusion in the measure.
2. The 'scaling', measurement, or valuation of these dimensions.
3. Some ethically appropriate rule for aggregating individual valuations determined in the scaling process.

We assume for the purposes of this chapter that the first step has been accomplished, so that we can concentrate now on what methods might be used to get people to reveal their preferences concerning the measurement, or more strongly, the evaluation of health/quality-of-life states. In undertaking to do this there is a clear presumption that health states can be quantified in various ways. Surveying the field of health status and quality-of-life measurement it is clear that significant change in recent times has occurred here: serious efforts have been made at conceptualising health status in ways that make this concept amenable to quantitative measurement. Some indication of this appeared in Chapter 2 where the development of health status measures was outlined. What is perhaps a little surprising is that modern measurement theory in the form of scaling dates back only to the 1940s. In the first part of this chapter we will look at the nature of measurement and the techniques of scaling.

MEASUREMENT

Measurement in essence means assigning numbers to aspects of objects or events according to various rules. Four kinds of scales can be distinguished: nominal, ordinal, interval and ratio. Nominal measurement refers to what in everyday parlance we would call 'numbering', for example of players in a football team. In the health context this type of measurement could be used to compare one medical intervention with another, for example classifying persons as 'died' or 'survived'. Evidently Florence Nightingale with her 'dead'/'relieved'/'unrelieved' classification was in favour of nominal measurement (see Chapter 2)! This is a rather limited form of measurement since it is little more than a system of classification. The procedure should not be belittled, though, since an assignment rule is in force and this is better than a random collection of entities. Nevertheless, as we are continually pointing out in this book, the world of measurement has moved on in its applications to health and health measurement.

Ordinal measurement is about the 'determination of greater or less': here the concern is with rank ordering. Examples would be hardness of minerals, grades of wool, even street numbers if these were measured sequentially, say moving away from a city centre. Thus we may describe health states by classifying them into, say: perfect health, moderate health, poor health, and seriously ill. Then assign numbers, say 1, 2, 3, 4 respectively. Now there is a rank ordering with '4' being the 'worst' health state here, but with no attempt being made to judge how much worse state 4 is over state 3 over state 2, etc. The 'how much' judgement would require what is called *cardinal measurement*. The interval and ratio scales aim to provide such a form of measurement.

Comparison can be made on cardinal scales using the arithmetic operations of addition and subtraction on an interval scale plus multiplication in the ratio scale case. On an interval scale items are scale ordered and incorporate a procedure for equating intervals or differences. An example will indicate that this is a simpler concept than it appears from the jargon. Take temperature in Celsius: it is clear that the difference between 20°C and 30°C is twice the difference between 5°C and 10°C but it cannot be said that 30°C is 'three times as hot' as 10°C. To appreciate this, note that the equivalent Fahrenheit temperatures in the latter comparison are 86°F and 50°F. The same entity – temperature – is being measured but since Celsius and Fahrenheit are only interval scales they do not have the ratio properties allowing the 'three times as hot' comparison to be made. The reason for this is that the zero on an interval scale is arbitrarily fixed and has no meaning in itself. In the health status context the same reasoning applies. The difference between 20 and 30 on an interval-based health status scale is the same as the difference between 10 and 20, but a person would not be judging 30 to be three times as good (bad) as 10.

It follows from what has been said that it ought to be possible to transform an interval scale into a ratio scale by defining a zero which is not arbitrary. And indeed this can be done for temperature in the form of the Rankine or Kelvin scales, each of which have an 'absolute zero'. Length, loudness and brightness are other examples of ratio scales. Now for health status it would be necessary to define a zero or at least a fixed 'reference' point such that a health status value of, say, 20 would be twice 'as good' or 'as bad' (depending on the direction of measurement of course!) as 10 on the scale. Unfortunately, and health measurement may well be an area where this applies, even the achievement of a ratio scale may not be very meaningful within a decision-making context. Thus although two miles is certainly twice one mile it may not be perceived as such by those contemplating a journey!

From the point of view of health evaluation cardinal scaling is required to answer the question 'how much more effective is one health intervention over another?' A ratio form of cardinal scale is desirable in assessing questions concerning how much better proportionately is one intervention over another. This has clear implications for resource allocation since it may help us to answer questions concerning what amounts of resources should be allocated to alternative interventions.

Many health status measures have been constructed using the measurement or scaling procedures outlined here, although only a few ratio scales have been developed. Disputes have arisen over the precise scaling properties of particular health status instruments, especially over whether certain measures do indeed have the ratio properties claimed for them. This is a matter of some importance given the resource allocation consideration mentioned in the previous paragraph. We will not review the debate. Instead an outline of the available scaling techniques will be presented, techniques which are dependent on the nature of measurement just discussed.

How can health state valuations be derived? What we are looking for are a measurement instrument or instruments in which preferences can be quantified in a valid and reliable manner, thus meeting the methodological requirements outlined in Chapter 3. Whose values might be used in evaluation or scaling will be considered later in the chapter. A number of techniques have been employed in health status measurement, the most popular being: category scaling, magnitude estimation, the standard gamble, and the time trade-off method. We shall also briefly consider the willingness-to-pay and equivalence methods. The term 'raters' will be used for those persons requested to do the scaling using these techniques. An earlier publication reviewed the literature on scaling methods in some detail: much of the commentary relates to this literature (Brooks, 1991).

Category Scaling (CS)

Other terms used for variants of this technique are category rating (CR) and rating scale (RS). The term 'visual analogue scale' (VAS) is often also used when category scaling is employed, although use of the VAS term is not confined to this method. The basic feature of these related methods is the presentation to raters of a scale in the form of a line, often taking on the appearance of a thermometer, which has clearly defined endpoints, say 0 and 1 or 0 and 100. These endpoints are 'fixed' in the sense that one end of the scale should represent the least preferred or 'worst' health status to the rater and the other endpoint should indicate the most preferred or 'best'. Typical endpoints are 'normal healthy life' and 'dead'. The latter of course can hardly be termed a 'health' state! The treatment of 'dead' in health status measurement instruments remains controversial, and there is also plenty of evidence to suggest that 'dead' is not the worst state for a lot of raters (Sintonen, 1981; Torrance, 1984).

With these endpoints in place, all suggested intermediate health states (descriptions of which are provided by the instrument developers) are then placed on the line by the rater in such a way that the intervals between these health states correspond to the differences in preferences as perceived by the rater. This would mean that the rater views a change in health status from 40 to 50 on his or her scale as equivalent to a change from 70 to 80, thus meeting at least the interval scale requirement that intervals or differences be equated. Practical ways of aiding raters in their task include using a thermometer with a 0–100 scale mounted on a felt background with sticks labelled with health state descriptions that are placed by the rater at the appropriate points next to the thermometer. A typical version of such a category scale is shown in Figure 5.1.

This type of scale can be used for scaling chronic health states. The rater should be told the age of onset of the chronic condition and the age of death and the chronic state(s) should be viewed as permanent from the age of onset to the age of death. Temporary health states can also be measured using this method: raters are faced with temporary states with specified time durations, after which normal health would ensue.

Category scaling ought, then, to provide at least an interval scale and thus cardinal measurement. It has been quite widely used, perhaps its most attractive feature being the visual nature of the approach which can help raters see what is expected of them. Even so, health measure users may still be faced with some difficulties in explaining to potential raters the precise nature of the exercise required of them. If particular studies make use of postal questionnaires these difficulties may be even more apparent and lead to poor response rates. Empirical studies have exposed a number of potential defects with the category methods. One possibility is response spreading, where raters appear to desire to use each category (i.e. each labelled health state) on the scale equally often, thus spreading out ratings when the health states might actually be close together. Alternatively raters may push particular states together when their 'true' values are far apart. Another problem, by no means confined to this technique, is the 'framing' problem where scale values may be crucially dependent on the precise way in which questions are asked of raters. Other difficulties relate to the scale and its endpoints, so that values assigned by raters may be influenced by the nature of the endpoints. It seems clear from empirical evidence, for example, that not all heath states can be placed on a continuum with perfect health at one end and death at the other. It may be worth stressing that what this method and all the other methods are essentially about is teasing out or discovering the 'true' values that people assign to health states and this is not an inherently straightforward task: health is a complex matter surrounded by much emotion. The problems in dealing with the conceptual framework for the per-

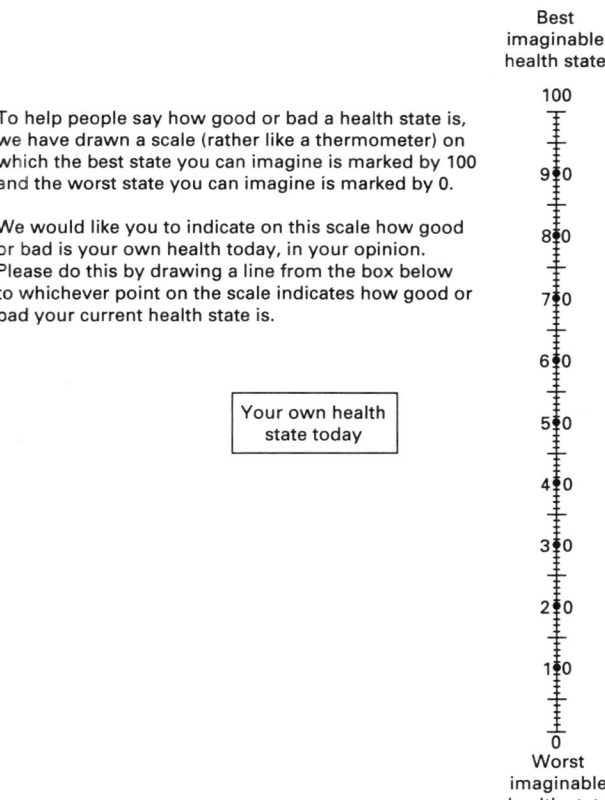

Figure 5.1 Euroqol own health state measure

Source: Williams, 1993.

ception of health and the valuation of health states will be further analysed in Chapter 7.

Finally on category scaling we may note first that studies using the technique should be required to meet the methodological requirements outlined in Chapter 3. Second, since the technique yields an interval rather than a ratio scale, its applicability for some types of health evaluation and thus for resource allocation, may be limited.

Magnitude Estimation (ME)

This method would appear to be a close cousin of the CS method, although that has not stopped family warfare breaking out over the respective virtues and drawbacks of the two methods! In the ME method a rater is given a standard reference state – for our purposes a health state description – which serves as a fixed point or state so that another state can be described as, say, 'twice as bad' or 'half as good' depending on the rater's preference judgements. The attempt to develop a ratio scale is evident in one of the early health status measurement efforts. Patrick *et al* (1973) gave the following instructions to raters using a reference state of 1000:

> Evaluate the desirability of each day by writing in the score box a number which reflects how preferable each day seems to you. This standard item describes a day which has been given a score of 1000. It is a day in the life of a person who was as healthy as possible on that day. Every other day should be scored in relation to this standard description. For example, if the item seems half as desirable as the standard, then write in the score of 500. If the day appears a tenth as preferable as the standard, then write in a score of 100. You may use any whole number or fraction that is greater than zero and equal to or less than 1000.

ME advocates claim this technique is superior to CS since it produces a ratio scale by asking raters to focus on proportions – the relationships between health states are explicitly subject to multiplication and division. It might be advocated, therefore, that resources flow proportionally to medical interventions as evaluated by the ME method.

One difficulty that seems to arise with the method is a seeming unwillingness on the part of some practitioners to rely on one fixed point: should zero appear in there somewhere? The answer, if a ratio scale is to be defined, is 'only if zero means none'! Of some interest is the derivation by Haig *et al.* (1986) of an 'illness index': these authors have defined and produced empirically a zero scale value which represents the absence of dysfunction and discomfort. Thus there is no requirement to anchor the upper part or 'worst end' of the scale: however 'bad' an illness state is can be judged numerically by the rater. This would appear to produce a ratio scale. Does this proposal herald a new era of 'illness status measurements' in health evaluation? There is little evidence of this so far, although Haig and his associates continue to work with this approach (Haig *et al.*, 1989).

The Standard Gamble (SG)

This technique is a favourite of those who insist on a 'firm theoretical base' for preference measurement. This base lies in the axioms of utility theory whose antecedents lie in the works of Jeremy Bentham from the early nineteenth century and which were articulated in 'modern' form most notably by von Neumann and Morgenstern (1944). 'Utility' refers essentially to the satisfaction to be gained from activities as broadly defined as one wishes.

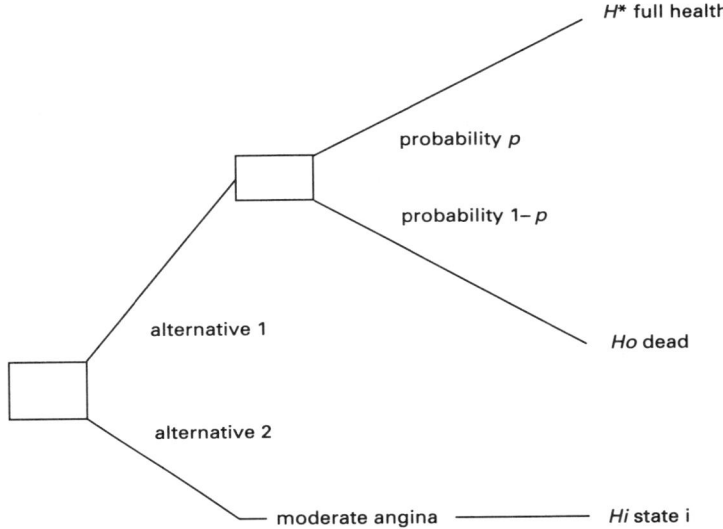

Figure 5.2 Standard gamble for a chronic health state preferred to death

Source: Adapted from Torrance, 1986.

Health care certainly generates utility: some of it will be process utility as a person feels better in the course of treatment, and hopefully lots of utility will be derived from the outcomes of medical interventions. (Of course medical treatment is often unpleasant, this being described in the utility framework by the unlovely term 'disutility'.) The modern terminology refers to 'expected' utility.

The first thing to note is that the approach is explicitly probabilistic – it addresses the question of how to conceptualise risk in decision-taking, which would seem to be eminently sensible in the medical world with which we are concerned. Let us start with two reference outcomes in the form of health states, one favourable (H^*), the other unfavourable (Ho). The health state rater is then faced with two scenarios:

1. The lottery: outcome H^* with probability p attached and outcome Ho with probability $1 - p$.
2. The certain outcome Hi, a state intermediate between H^* and Ho.

Probability p is then varied until the rater is indifferent between the two alternatives, thus giving the preference or utility value for Hi of $Hi = p$.

Consider Figure 5.2: suppose heart surgery would result in full health or death and that the alternative in the absence of surgery would be moderate angina. A rater may turn out to be indifferent between surgery giving a 90 per cent chance of full health and a 10 per cent chance of death, and the certainty of moderate angina. This means of course that the rater thinks that 'taking a gamble' at these odds (probabilities) is viewed as being on a par with being in the health state of moderate angina. If we 'normalise' to a utility index on a 0 to 1 scale then it should be evident that $U(H^*) = 1$, $U(Ho) = 0$, and $U(Hi) = p$. The last value perhaps needs a little further explanation. In the example we had 90 per cent/10 per cent from surgery as equivalent to angina: the normalised value for $Hi = 0.9$. Suppose another rater considered 80 per cent/20 per cent as equivalent in his or her view to angina, then it is apparent that it is the 80 per cent we now look to for the preference value of the latter person ($Hi = 0.8$); this is the value at which the individual becomes indifferent between the two scenarios.

Note that this technique is as 'neutral' as the other approaches in the sense that *for the purposes of health status measurement* we are asking raters to rate scenarios, we are not asking them to make the actual decisions, or even for that matter to put themselves into the shoes of the decision-maker! We are asking them for their evaluations of health states in risk-laden situations. It should be stated, however, that there is a huge field of decision analysis (Bell *et al.*, 1988; Kassirer *et al.*, 1987) in which actual decisions are at issue: we are concentrating here on health state scaling.

What can we say about the standard gamble technique? If it appears rather complex this is probably because it is! Studies give conflicting reports concerning the abilities of raters to comprehend the tasks required of them. Indeed some writers are quite scathing about the meaningfulness or otherwise of confronting people with precise quantitative probabilistic statements. What does it actually mean, they ask, to talk about a reduction in the probability of death from say, surgery, by 10 per cent? What are we expecting of people in asking them to make judgements or quantify preferences about health states in this manner? Is it appropriate to ask raters to judge these life/death situations when they are not directly involved in the decisions?

On the other hand the world is a risky place. Those using the SG approach stress the necessity to address this reality, and are convinced of the worthwhileness of this technique, especially since, to reiterate an earlier point, it is grounded in an established tried-and-tested theoretical framework. Recent developments in decision theory, backed up by various pieces of empirical work, are, however, casting strong doubt on the hegemony of expected utility theory as *the* approach to decision-making.

We will not review these developments in detail but their flavour can be judged from *regret* theory. This suggests that people may regret or rejoice in the decisions they make, thus losing or gaining more utility than predicted by the expected utility approach. The regret-rejoice approach would appear particularly apposite in the medical context where decisions may turn out to give quite different levels of satisfaction/utility than those measured by the standard gamble approach to evaluation. This ought in many cases to be evident after the event! The challenge for the regret theorists is somehow to predict the levels of regret and rejoicing before the event. Note also that regret theory is dependent on the notion that regret (or rejoicing) follows from making a choice – but in clinical decision-making the patient may not (or at least not fully) be making the choice (Loomes, 1988).

Such theorising about decision-making engenders much controversy, as might be imagined, but given our emphasis on change it is certainly appropriate to point to the clear possibility that such developments may result in substantial changes in how health status is measured, especially within the utility framework, and in the ways in which medical decision-making is conceptualised and viewed.

Time Trade-Off (TTO)

This method takes a slightly different tack from the other techniques, although it is still concerned with scaling raters' preferences. The method explicitly views health status as a concept encompassing time durations rather than just point-of-time health assessments. It can be used for a chronic health state considered better than death, a chronic health state considered worse than death and in eliciting preferences for temporary health states. The various time-related choices are thus made quite explicit. Take the health-state-rated-better-than-death scenario. Here the rater is faced with, say, two alternatives:

(a) Chronic state hi for time t, where t is the life expectancy of an individual with this chronic condition, followed by death.
(b) Healthy for a period of time x, which is less than t, followed by death.

As with the standard gamble method we need to determine the preference values – this is accomplished by varying the time period x until the rater is indifferent between the two alternatives. This gives a value for health state hi equal to x/t. The TTO method is illustrated in Figure 5.3.

Advocates of this technique point to the pervasiveness of trade-offs in evaluation and actual decision-making and the flexibility of the method. It is clear that it is possible to look at a variety of trade-off scenarios, as indicated in the previous paragraph. Potential drawbacks of the method are

1. It is relatively time-consuming to administer, although some researchers suggest that is simpler to administer than the standard gamble method.
2. The method lacks the theoretic properties of lottery-based techniques thus failing to incorporate in an explicit manner raters' attitudes towards uncertainty, although, as indicated earlier, these properties may be open to question anyway.

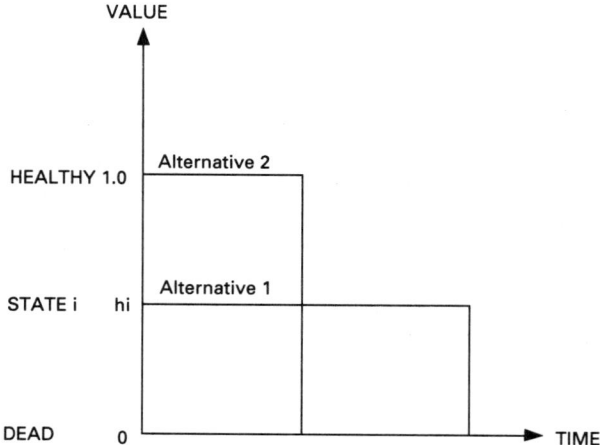

Figure 5.3 Time trade-off for a chronic health state preferred to death

Source: Torrance, 1986.

3. The technique proceeds on the assumption that raters' perceptions of time are linear – one year is much the same as another – which may simply not be the case.

Equivalence

Here the rater has to decide how many people in one health state are equivalent to a specified number of people in another health state (Froberg and Kane, 1989b). This would allow the comparison of, for example, how many patients should be cured of a particular disease in order for this to be equivalent to the cure a specified number of patients with another disease. This rather interesting approach has not been widely used, perhaps because such comparisons are viewed as offensive or unrealistic. As with many of the issues raised in this book concerning health measurement the rejoinder would be that actual decisions might well conform to something like that postulated in this approach so is it not better therefore to examine explicitly whether this is the case? (Mulley, 1989). As ever, though, valid and reliable measurement methods are required.

Willingness to Pay

This technique has also been employed as a way of measuring health preferences, although its use would be more widely recognised as belonging to cost-benefit analysis, rather than the cost-utility analysis framework in which much of the application of health status measurement for evaluative purposes currently lies, since monetary values are assigned to these preferences. Raters are asked what they would be willing to pay to provide a complete cure for a disease such as rheumatoid arthritis, or, more commonly, what they would be willing to pay to reduce the risk of incurring particular diseases or conditions. Such questions seem to give more plausible results if people are asked about the proportions of their incomes they are willing to pay, rather than the absolute sums of money, thus avoiding the criticism that the rich would likely give higher valuations (Thompson, 1986). A major difficulty with this method at the moment is that little is known about the methodological 'robustness' of the approach (Mulley, 1989).

Some economists, however, argue that the method *is* robust from the economic theory point of view since it originates from various strands of welfare economics. Determined efforts are being made to give cost-benefit analysis its due in health evaluation and as a consequence there has been something of a recent revival in willingness-to-pay studies (Gafni, 1991).

It will be apparent from this outline review of scaling that there are many substantive issues still to be resolved in the application of the available techniques to health status and quality of life measurement. Two most helpful 'position' papers are those of Froberg and Kane (1989b,d): they examine the scaling methods in the light of the standard methodological criteria, and recommend further research on the reliability and validity of scaling methods, with particular emphasis on how health-state preferences are formed. This they deem of importance because of the trend towards social preference valuation within the context of global (generic) health measurement and the use of such measurement in the cost-utility evaluation framework. One of the major measurement approaches to emerge has been the quality-adjusted life-year, to which we now turn our attention.

Quality-Adjusted Life-Years (QALYs)

Any explanation of developments in the evaluative aspects of health status measurement is bound to address the construction of QALYs. As with other aspects of measurement and evaluation there are fads and fashions, and it would appear that QALYs are currently in fashion, if not universally acclaimed! The first formal use of the term 'quality-adjusted life year' should probably be attributed to Weinstein and Stason in 1977. The appearance of their article on cost-effectiveness in a major medical journal, namely, *The New England Journal of Medicine*, was an indication of the rising interest at that time in health evaluation from a broader standpoint than the purely or mainly medical, and undoubtedly helped enhance this interest. They argued that QALYs could be used as an outcome measure in cost-effectiveness analysis and explicitly used the term 'cost per quality-adjusted year of life saved' as a cost-effectiveness measure. They also traced this type of measurement to the health indices developed in the early 1970s by, *inter alia*, Bush and his colleagues (with their concept of a 'well-year', Kaplan *et al.*, 1976) and Torrance and his associates (with their strong emphasis on utility measures, Torrance *et al.*, 1972). Chapter 2 described some of these developments. The term QALY subsequently became a common part of the evaluative vocabulary, and many analysts would now place QALY calculations under the rubric of cost-utility analysis.

In one sense there need be little controversy over the QALY concept. We noted in Chapter 1 that health interventions are not solely, or even very often, a matter of life and death: they are normally about restoring health and all this entails – this whole book is concerned with the fundamental issue of why and how health status measurement has been subject to such significant changes in the last 45 years or so. Ask any medical gathering whether one year of life is much the same as any other and a resounding chorus of 'no' is usually to be heard. It is not just the quantity of life but also the quality of life which concerns people, medical professionals or otherwise. This applies just as much, of course, to the life-years saved in the life-and-death situations as to those interventions explicitly concerned with changing morbidity and raising health status. So it can probably be agreed that the measurement of quality of life is a necessary part of health evaluation. The significant issues surround the way in which this is to be achieved. In particular in the present context, do QALYs as presently constituted add, in an appropriate way, to our evaluative capacities? QALYs are controversial and the criteria for assessing 'appropriateness' are worth reviewing. We shall return to these matters in Chapter 7.

How are QALYs constructed? In principle any of the scaling methods described in this chapter can provide a basis. What these methods have in common is that they each allow the derivation of 'scores' for different health states which are comparable between these states, and indeed are cardinally measurable, some on interval scales and others on ratio scales. Two dimensions are used: life-expectancy or life-years and a quality adjustment to these life years. A life-saving operation will mean a patient can be expected to live an additional number of years, which then need to 'quality-adjusted'. This is often accomplished by standardising onto a scale of 0 to 1. If someone is deemed to be in a heath state which has been calibrated, that is, scored by raters at a value of 0.5, then each expected life-year will be given a QALY value of 0.5. In measuring the outcomes of health interventions (not confined to life-saving procedures, note), 'productivity' is the difference over a period of time between expected QALYs with a particular intervention and without it. For whole programmes this would of course require the summation of QALYs accruing to individuals. Figure 5.4 provides a pictorial representation of the QALY in the health intervention context.

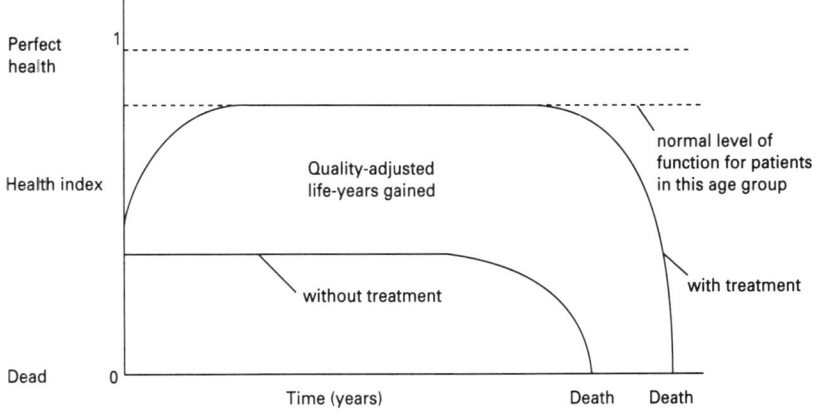

Figure 5.4 Quality-adjusted life-years added by treatment

Source: Drummond, 1989.

Thus the QALY essentially provides a common denominator by which to compare alternative health programmes and interventions. The QALYs generated by an intervention can then be compared with the resources used, preferably socially evaluated, so that (social) costs/QALY can be calculated, often within the cost-utility analysis framework. We shall consider in Chapter 7 the usefulness or otherwise of approaching health sector resource allocation using QALYs.

Healthy Year Equivalents (HYEs)

One reaction to the development of QALYs will now be outlined. Gafni and Birch (1993) have argued that for the purposes of economic evaluation, in particular cost-utility analysis, certain properties of an outcome measure are required. First, for a measure of outcome to be consistent with welfare economics theory it has to be related to utility theory. Second, a measure should fully reflect the internal structure of an individual's preference formulation. Third, individuals' attitudes to risk must be incorporated. Finally, equity considerations are an intrinsic part of outcome measurement.

These authors give low marks to QALYs on conformity with these properties. They and their colleagues have developed the HYE (healthy year equivalent) in an attempt to meet their stated criteria in outcome measurement (Mehrez and Gafni, 1991). The method involves finding a hypothetical combination of the number of years in full health that is equivalent, in terms of the individual's utility, to living a number of years in a health state rated at less than full health. A two-stage standard gamble procedure is used to produce the HYE values, thus incorporating risk. It is claimed that the method combines the two outcomes – quality of life and quantity of life – which are essential for economic evaluation. Since the method is derived from utility theory under uncertainty it can, according to its developers, generate a community health-related well-being measure based on the theoretical foundations of welfare economic theory. It can also be adjusted for equity as required.

These claims remain to be tested in any detail, although a literature largely peopled by economists is developing (Buckingham, 1993; Culyer and Wagstaff, 1993; Gafni et al., 1993). The investment of considerable intellectual capital in QALYs ensures that the debate will be an intense one!

Saved Young Life Equivalent (SAVE)

From Norway comes another reaction to some of the perceived problems of QALYs: the saved young life equivalent or SAVE (Nord, 1992). This is defined as the value assigned by society to saving the life of a young person and restoring him or her to full health. Nord argues that his measure could be used as an aid in decisions concerning the allocation of resources across health programmes. This measure is undoubtedly to be placed alongside the QALY and the HYE within the social value tradition that began with the attempts to develop generic measures of the aggregate variety.

WHOSE VALUES?

Finally in this chapter an important issue, highly germane to the measurement process, and one that has generated considerable debate, requires consideration. The neutral term 'raters' has been employed thus far in this chapter. The natural question arises: who should do the rating? If we consider who puts the 'quality' into the QALY, the debate concerns whether the health status weights be based on citizens' preferences, experts' judgements, or decision-makers' (perhaps politicians') judgements, or any combination thereof, without suggesting for one moment that decision-makers are not citizens! We need not worry about the precise definition of those who might be deemed members of the 'experts' category: these are often taken to be health 'professionals' but could just as easily encompass anybody with a professional interest in health matters.

But, now, where do patients themselves come into the picture, apart from being part of the citizenry? Should their particular interests be addressed? This latter question may seem a self-evidently foolish one, given that medical care, for example, is everything to do with patients and their welfare. The problem is that it is not self-evident that a sample of patients is appropriate for the generation of a set of 'social' weights for health conditions/ states, but neither is it self-evident that any other group would produce more valid weightings. By 'social' here we are referring to valuations that are deemed to be relevant for judging the allocation and distribution of resources from a socially optimal viewpoint. We may of course wish to relate this to the notion of social quality of life, as outlined in Chapter 4.

There are some tricky issues here. Suppose we ask a doctor to rate a patient on a particular scale, say one concerned with physical limitations. The doctor rates these limitations as 'moderate' or, to quantify this judgement, 0.3 on a rising scale of limitations from 0 to 1. What does the doctor actually mean by this? Now of course the doctor may well have received instruction in scaling, but suppose the patient concerned, under the same instructions, judges his limitations to be 'moderate' and scores himself at 0.4. Does this matter? Certainly, if we wish to make quantitative (and cardinal, see the early part of this chapter) calculations about health status. In addition, and perhaps more important, do the perceptions of the health states (physical limitations in this case) themselves mean the same thing to the two parties? (Note that both have rated the patient's state as 'moderate'.) This is a well-known difficulty in philosophy, psychology and economics.

Let us explore the issue further. Some authors have suggested that self-ratings are limited by their subjectivity. An individual may wish to please the doctor and thus exaggerate his or her ability to function. Or the patient may claim to be worse than he or she really is, perhaps to gain a more sympathetic hearing. It is also observed that persons experiencing chronic illness such as arthritis adapt to their conditions, thus subjectively (as of course is required of them) valuing the same (descriptive) health states differently over time. These considerations seem to imply that the proposition, articulated by some observers, that it is the patients' valuations that should be paramount in health state assessment since they are the ones experiencing the (ill-health) conditions, has certain shortcomings.

At the same time professional ratings can be subject to bias. Three points can be made.

1. The doctor may carry over an impression of the person's function from one rating to the next in order to make the ratings consistent.
2. A rater may upgrade the functional ability scores if a patient is believed to be a 'complainer'. This may be appropriate in given circumstances but clearly raises questions of how to disentangle bias from ratings.
3. Imprecision may occur when different raters use different frames of reference in grading functional ability. This could apply in the doctor: patient case and also in professional: professional evaluations.

Extensive evidence of patient and professional perceptions of health-related quality of life has been reviewed by Fitzpatrick (1993).

An interesting development in recent years goes under the title of *judgement analysis*. This framework has wider relevance than the 'whose values' issue but is worth discussion at this juncture. There are a number of problems associated with judgement (Joyce, 1983).

1. Two observers of a common set of data might make different uses of the same information, thus disagreeing in their judgements.
2. A judge can seldom fully represent, even to himself or herself, *(i)* what information he or she is using in arriving at a judgement, and *(ii)* the way in which he or she differentially weights this information in collating it to form a judgement.
3. Even if a judge is fully aware of all the information, he or she will tend to use it inconsistently, for example by giving small weight to one factor on one occasion and more on another, even when the two situations are identical. Substitute 'rater' for 'observer' and for 'judge' and we can see the potential relevance of this analysis for health status rating or scaling.

These kinds of problems would appear to support the view that sole reliance on medical professional evaluations in health scaling should be treated with circumspection. Interestingly, various techniques have been developed under the rubric of clinical judgement analysis to try to improve clinical judgement. On the other hand it is worth making an important point in favour of doctors' judgements, and that is that they have 'been here before': they do normally have experience of thousands of cases and thus ought to have well-informed views, especially of health status, if perhaps not of the wider quality-of-life aspects of their patients. In other words, the argument goes, they may have better knowledge of what is likely to happen to the health of the patient, but only the patient can judge what that change means to him or her in quality-of-life terms.

Further, we can look at a number of issues that have been raised in what has often proved to be a lively debate. First there is unhappiness that 'quality adjustment', i.e. scaling, be based on asking healthy people to rate particular health states incorporating particular ill-health conditions (Avorn, 1984). It is argued that this is invalid and therefore it is indefensible to compare such valuations with valuations collected for a truly disabled population. A related point is that valuations arising from particular sample groups, say the young, may prove grossly misleading if these are then used to draw conclusions about resource allocation for, say, the elderly. Another possibility is that variability in valuations from patient to patient could be much greater than differences from condition to condition. On the other hand, differences in valuations attributable to the personal characteristics of raters may be trivial compared with the differences that might arise from the different scaling techniques in the first place (Boyle and Torrance, 1984).

It would probably be foolhardy to draw definitive conclusions on the 'whose values?' question. It is hard, though, to escape the conclusion that everybody ought to be in there somewhere if we are to obtain social valuations! Posing the question to medical students once produced the answer 'an opinion poll', an answer which certainly captures the essence of the issue if we do indeed wish to generate social valuations. If scaling can be undertaken using a representative, appropriately randomised and stratified, sample of the populace then this could in principle deliver a set of social weights to be used in evaluating health interventions. This is a big 'if', of course, and obtaining a good response rate may prove difficult. Nevertheless some groups of health status measurement workers, including amongst their number the author of this book, have been experimenting in this direction.

As part of the work of the Euroqol Group (1990), which comprises seven centres in five European countries, the Swedish Institute for Health Economics tested a standardised non-disease-specific instrument for describing and valuing health-related quality of life (Brooks *et al.*, 1991). Visual analogue scales of the thermometer type – essentially a form of category scaling – were used to rank a given set of health states formulated by the Group. In the context of the present discussion the interesting feature of the exercise is that questionnaires were sent to 1000 people randomly selected to provide a representative sample of the Swedish population aged 16–84 years. A total of 349 persons responded and 208 provided sufficient information for detailed quantitative analysis of their health status valuations. These response rates were disappointing, but a determined effort was made to obtain social valuations, and our experience indicates that it is possible to run surveys of this type. The health valuations that resulted from this survey indicated a striking similarity with those of Euroqol studies in Frome (England) and Bergen op Zoom (the Netherlands): see Table 5.1. The Euroqol Group continues to explore health status measurement from its common methodology.

Despite what has just been written it would be wrong to concentrate solely on the attempts that have been made to generate social weights. There is undoubtedly scope for a more 'micro' level of health status measurement; one thinks particularly, for example, of the disease-specific measures, where a strong case can be made for concentrating on patient and professional valuations. Such measures could then have considerable relevance for resource allocation and 'value-for-money' considerations in particular circumstances, not least in helping to inform clinical decision-making.

CONCLUDING REMARKS

This chapter has surely shown that the seemingly innocuous term 'measurement' takes on an unsuspected complexity when subjected to detailed analysis! The techniques described and issues raised are of importance. We started

Table 5.1 Euroqol: results of three pilot studies

Health state	Median Valuations			Mean Valuations			Standard Deviations		
	Lund	Frome	BoZ	Lund	Frome	BoZ	Lund	Frome	BoZ
111111	100	99	95	93	95	93	13	10	13
111121	86	84	86	83	81	81	16	14	19
111112	75	70	75	69	67	71	21	18	22
111122	70	68	70	64	65	69	20	17	21
112121	65	70	65	61	67	63	22	18	23
112131	50	59	60	51	56	56	21	19	22
112222	35	40	43	36	41	43	20	17	21
112232	35	35	33	36	36	37	20	17	23
212232	22	25	20	26	26	26	20	16	20
222232	10	10	7	14	12	12	19	12	15
232232	7	5	6	12	8	10	19	9	16
322232	4	2	5	9	5	10	18	7	13
332232	1	1	4	8	4	7	19	6	12
being dead	0	0	3	10	10	19	24	20	25

Lund: Sweden (n= 208/1000)
Frome: United Kingdom (n= 310/1321)
Bergen op Zoom: Netherlands (n= 74/200)

Health states are composites of dimensions (mobility, self-care, pain, etc.) and levels of these dimensions, where '1' is the 'highest' ranking or level.

Source: Adapted from Euroqol Group, 1990.

by considering the nature of measurement itself and pointed to the key features of the cardinal approach in health status measurement, not least in providing the sort of health state valuations which are required for evaluation and for potential resource allocation. We then moved on to the different scaling approaches which have been tried and applied: this is an essential consideration because health status (and quality of life) needs to be valued in some way. There is now a huge literature on health scaling, ranging from continuing analysis of the scaling process – especially the pros and cons of the alternative techniques – to the widespread application of these measures in the health field.

Finally we investigated the thorny question of whose values should be used in the scaling process. As was observed, there are no easy answers to this question. Issues ranging from clinical judgement to patient perception are raised in this context. Considerable work is being undertaken in the area of social weights, one example being the programme of the Euroqol Group. Equally, the use of patient and professional values in the disease-specific measures appears quite justifiable.

We can conclude by repeating that those who are in favour of quantitative measurement in addition to qualitative judgement have to justify their approach – this means producing methodologically sound ways of evaluating health status which have the potential to be used to inform decision-making in a variety of contexts.

CHAPTER 6

Implications for Decision-Making

We now have in place a reasonably comprehensive picture of the nature and development of health status measurement. At the outset attempts were made to answer the question concerning why health status measurement has proceeded apace in recent years. This was followed by an historical outline of the developments in health status measurement, combined with a classification and description of the nature of some of the measures themselves. It was then stressed that there are certain key methodological requirements if health status measures are to be treated seriously in health measurement and evaluation: in particular such measures should be statistically 'sound', reliable and valid. Before considering the actual measurement processes appropriate to health status assessment a tour was taken around the issue of quality, and as we saw this turned out be a complex and indeed often elusive concept or set of concepts. Finally measurement was considered from first principles through to the controversies surrounding whose values should be used in health status measurement.

It is now time to consider the implications of all this for decision-making. A moment's thought will indicate that a huge area is opened up for contemplation since decision-making runs from a person worried about his or her health deciding to seek medical advice through to a government making decisions on the allocations of large sums of money to the health sector. Indeed even this range of possibilities fails adequately to capture other areas for decision such as the promotion of good health and the prevention of ill health. So what role has health status measurement to play in decision-making at the different levels and in the various sectors of health and medicine? Has this role been changing over the years, and what happens next? These are some of the questions to be explored in these last two chapters. More specifically the following topics will be addressed in this chapter: the relationships between health services research – in this context research into health status measures, quality of life and decision analysis – and decision-making; clinical trials and health status measurement; medical ethics and health status measurement; clinical decision-making; prevention, promotion, and health status measurement. This constitutes a formidable range of topics. The emphasis, though, at all times in what follows will be on the links between health status measurement and the facets of medicine and health

HEALTH SERVICES RESEARCH AND DECISION-MAKING

care under consideration and, where applicable, the changing nature of these links.

Let us start with an excellent survey of the issues by Berwick (1988) whose analysis of quality measurement as research was used in Chapter 4. It might be worth pointing out that Dr Berwick's credentials at the time of writing this paper were Vice President for Quality-of-Care Measurement, Harvard Community Health Plan, and Associate Professor of Pediatrics at Harvard Medical School. Why, he asks, is there such a gap between what is now an enormous research effort on quality measurement (including of course what we have been terming health status measurement) and the day-to-day workings of the health sector? His answers are instructive and although the context is the United States, his points are likely to have general applicability wherever formal quality assessment is taken seriously.

His first point is that quality measurements as presently constituted are rather slow to yield their conclusions, whereas health care decision-makers have to react quickly to changing events. The quality measures could be adapted to yield results in what he neatly calls 'managerially useful time periods' but by and large this has not been the case. Banta and Andreasen (1990) reinforce this point in a wider context: 'Politicians do not read scientific journals.' They suggest that the time lag in publication means that many technology assessments have lost their usefulness by the time they become accessible in published form.

Second, much of the quality assurance research has been at too aggregated a level. Large-scale studies of health care systems or dispersed groups of doctors or comparisons of performance across hospitals may not yield relevant or useful results for decision-making by the head of a department of medicine or an administrator of a health facility.

Third, quality measurement tends to be expensive but the resources made available for measurement tend to be very limited. Research results have somehow to be converted into relatively cheap measurement methods. Resources should be made available for such measurement and this would require formal commitment to the funding of quality measurement.

Fourth, lessons can be learned from the methods of quality control engineers about the appropriate modes of information display. Standardised charts and graphic displays are common in industrial control but 'virtually nonexistent in health care'. Health quality measures are currently presented in forms which 'are unlikely to be read, let alone used, by busy managers, impatient physicians, and technically unsophisticated purchasers of health care'. It strikes one in this context that, if every health facility and every general practitioner's office is to be 'computerised' or otherwise subjected to the charms of information technology, then there ought to be scope for the adoption of imaginative approaches to quality measurement in health sector decision-making right along to the level of the individual doctor.

Fifth, and this takes us back to some familiar themes from Chapter 4, Berwick refers to the 'tyranny of outcome'. According to him, outcome measurement is too predominant in quality assessment. Why does this pose problems? First, and a very familiar refrain indeed, are the often tenuous links between health care practices and health care results, particularly when it comes to choosing between alternative practices. This poses a dilemma for quality measurement. One result may be paralysis: not even to attempt to measure outcome. But there must be some value in present practices, both for doctors and patients, otherwise why persist with them? We are back to process. Patients may for example be seeking the sense of safety or being cared for that comes with good health care. To Berwick these are part of outcome also, but rarely appear in outcome assessment. In other words, there is more to health care than health.

He is also concerned with what he discerns as a tendency to go for a unidimensional view of quality. Our discussion in Chapter 4 indicates the limitations of such an approach. As Berwick points out, the unidimensional approach applied to the complexities of health care 'will almost certainly miss important lessons regarding multiple and independent attributes of the system' under study. For him the definition of quality cannot solely depend on the implicit standards of one set of professionals but depends essentially on the point of view of the person served and what he or she expects from health care. This of course conforms with the 'individualised' definition of quality (see Chapter 4) and does place a significant burden on the information and knowledge available to the patient/consumer. In passing it may be observed that if the unidimensional approach is to be criticised in this way, then some doubt might be cast on the QALY type of measurement, depending on one's views as to the comprehensiveness of such measurement in capturing quality. Further discussion of QALYs appears in Chapter 7.

Another matter concerning outcome raised by Berwick is that outcome may not be an efficient detector of quality problems. Again the 'industrial' model is used. A design or process may be flawed even if the flaw(s) have not yet produced a defective product. He claims that 'bad outcomes in health care are generally not frequent enough to be used to detect flaws in process or design'. Hence health care quality measurement must largely rely on methods which can judge the design and process of health systems. One is bound to ask, however: if we are not measuring outcomes in serious, systematic ways, then how can we judge what constitutes 'bad outcomes'?

Despite this critique, Berwick feels that outcome measurement as a component of quality assessment experienced significant technical advances during the decade prior to his article (written originally in 1986). He cites also the efforts of the Joint Commission for Accreditation of Health Care Organizations to generate outcome material (mentioned in Chapter 4) and the increased emphasis on peer review in the USA.

Outcome measurement has its part to play, therefore. Interestingly, amongst his prescriptions are:

1. That decision analysis and related disciplines will need to extend health status outcome 'into the psychosocial domains of effectiveness of importance to patients and physicians'.
2. That functional status assessment measures should be developed in versions that are both 'simple enough to incorporate into real-world data bases and yet valid enough to use in assessing care and case-mix'.
3. That advances in utility theory and the assessment of patients' preferences be used to shed light on the trade-offs among the different dimensions of quality.

All these concerns *are* being addressed by various researchers in health status measurement so the real questions concern how far Berwick's complaints about the gap between theory and practice are justified.

An editorial in the *Journal of the American Medical Association* (Flanagin and Lundberg, 1990) appears to support Berwick's worries, asking: 'Will formal decision-making methods also fall irretrievably between the cracks of academe and clinical reality?' The concept of 'clinical reality' is an interesting one! Presumably it refers to the 'hands-on' dealing with patients. Clinical decision-making will be considered in more detail below. The editorial suggests that everyone acknowledges that formal decision-making approaches will not replace individual clinical judgement. Nevertheless, the authors of the editorial are commending to the journal's readers a new regular column on clinical decision-making which they 'hope will help free decision theory from its restrictive academic base and provide a place for it in clinical reality'. Use is made later of material from this column. Despite the evident difficulties, it appears that the receptiveness of the medical profession to potential 'outside' influences on medical decision-making is on the increase.

CLINICAL TRIALS

We move now from consideration of the interface, or lack of it, between research on quality and health status and decision-making to a more detailed analysis of decision-making itself, commencing at the clinical level. We are interested in the links between health status measures and clinical decision-making and how, despite Berwick's strictures, these have developed in recent years. A prerequisite for this must be a (brief) discussion of the randomised controlled trial (RCT) procedure. Why? Because RCTs 'have become widely employed, well accepted, and generally regarded as the "gold standard" of cause-effect evaluation' (Feinstein, 1988) in the clinical context. The technique was first applied in medicine by the Medical Research Council (on the prompting of Austin Bradford Hill) in the late 1940s and the results published in the early 1950s, (Doll, 1992). The approach is to compare outcome in a group of patients randomly allocated to one form of treatment with that in another randomised group receiving another treatment or placebo. Then the hypothesis that one form of treatment is better than the other or than placebo, i.e. the treatment 'works', is tested. To reduce possible bias the 'double-blind' RCT was devised, in which neither the doctor nor the patients know which of the two treatments is being given.

Now in principle this approach could be applied to all medical and health care interventions. In practice there can be problems, as always, and there are ethical questions also. Practical problems include the numbers problem in the tests of significance which are used to differentiate between treatments or between treatment and placebo. With small numbers it is rather too easy to produce the result that treatment is no more effective than placebo. On the other hand a large sample may give statistically significant results but be clinically unimportant (Cochrane, 1972). For some conditions there may simply not be enough cases to mount an RCT, or the costs of achieving suitable samples may be inordinate.

On the ethical side there are some potentially profound difficulties. Some examples of these difficulties will be illustrated. First some procedures simply should not be subjected to RCTs. The criterion used for making such judgements appears to be medical consensus, based upon whatever procedures were originally used to derive such a consensus. One problem here of course is that the consensus may change. This raises the interesting question as to why the consensus changes: presumably as a result of increased knowledge? But then it may be RCTs which are required to acquire this knowledge, thus introducing an element of circularity, to say the least! Cochrane's (1972) examples of procedures unsuitable for RCTs are: surgery for lung cancer, cytological tests for prevention of cervical carcinoma, and dietetic therapy for phenylketonuria (PKU). 'No RCTs have ever been carried out to test the value of these standard therapies and tests.' Another good example is in breast cancer treatment where, in judging between lumpectomy and mastectomy, blind testing is not deemed appropriate. On the plus side, though, it ought to be noted that some interventions have been or are so obviously beneficial that RCTs are not required. Penicillin would presumably be a good example. The difficulties arise when no such 'easy' consensus is available.

A further point is that once medical innovations have actually been put into practice it is hardly ethical to deny patients what has come to be 'routine' treatment in order to mount a clinical trial. As Cochrane pointed out this means that there are sections of medicine whose effectiveness cannot be measured and thus the efficiency of the health sector may well be reduced.

Having said all this it is not impossible to bring about the abandonment of existing medical practices by demonstration through RCTs, a famous example being freezing the stomach in the treatment of gastric ulcer.

Elaborating on a point just made: what about the ethics of not administering the new treatment being tested to the 'control' sample of individuals in the trial? There is unease over the 'lottery' elements of the RCT so that the treatment which a particular patient gets is a matter of chance. The counter to this is that the RCT procedure simply reflects the inherent uncertainty over the outcomes of treatment anyway. More detailed consideration of medical ethics will be given below.

How does this discussion relate to health status measurement? Clearly RCTs are eminently applicable in the therapeutic context and have been extensively used in the testing of new drugs. Similarly, the procedure could be used in the testing of new technology, although apparently this is not so common. If the concern is with life-or-death issues and survival rates then the RCT can provide the mechanism for the judgement of the worthwhileness or otherwise of such medical interventions. But what about when quality of life is also at issue? Should health status measures be incorporated into the RCT procedure? There seems no reason why not. Indeed, and more positively, it could be argued that it is essential to do so when differences in the quality of life are likely to be the key discriminators between alternative health interventions. Unfortunately, and in the light of the ethical matters just raised, this might make the 'ethicality' of RCTs more problematical!

The sort of issue that can arise here is illustrated by Teeling Smith's (1988) claim that several medicines have been withdrawn from the market because of wide publicity about the risks involved whilst at the same time benefits were measured only in clinical terms. The recommended withdrawal of the arthritis drug Opren undoubtedly posed difficulties for rheumatologists whose patients felt they were benefiting from this particular drug. If 'hard' quantitative measures of benefits, particularly in terms of quality of life, had been available, the risks might have been deemed acceptable, Teeling Smith contends.

In this context it is worth returning to Cochrane (1972), ever the RCT enthusiast. For him RCTs should be used everywhere possible. He pointed out that Florence Nightingale suggested in 1858 that hospitals should do the sick no harm, but that the first controlled trial comparing home with hospital treatment was published in 1971, and the first controlled trial of length of stay and early mobilisation appeared in 1967. For him, therefore, all these aspects of the medical process should be evaluated in a controlled way, preferably using the RCT format. Now it should be evident that once we play on the wider field, moving beyond survival rates and therapeutic considerations, we will be in need of appropriate tactics, and these could well involve the use of formal health status and quality measures. It should be stated that Cochrane, who died in 1988 (within a few days of Thomas

McKeown, who for much of his career liked to look beyond the purely 'medical' model in explaining changes in health and health status), was ever-mindful of the economics of what he was proposing and used to stress the need for the proper costing of RCTs and for efficiency in the health sector, which for him had to include the appropriate use of the available resources.

MEDICAL ETHICS AND HEALTH STATUS MEASUREMENT

Ethical issues have already surfaced briefly. A more detailed treatment will now be assayed, although there is no pretence at comprehensiveness: we shall concentrate on the interface between ethics and health status measurement. As it happens there is a very useful treatment by Siegler (1987) of the relationships between decision analysis and medical ethics, so we will make use of this here.

Siegler regards what he calls 'clinical ethics' as a new discipline, one 'that aims to improve patient care and health professionals' satisfaction by identifying, analysing, and seeking to resolve the clinical, ethical, and legal considerations that confront patients, families, physicians, and clinical investigators in their interactions'. Clinical ethics is both an analytic and a descriptive approach to process and outcome in clinical decisions – our familiar terms once again! Particular emphases are laid on the doctor–patient and doctor–patient–institution relationships.

In contemplation of a patient 'case' there are four aspects to a decision strategy: *(i)* medical indications, *(ii)* informed patient preferences, *(iii)* quality of life considerations, and *(iv)* external factors. Medical decisions arise from the processes of diagnosis and prognosis which in turn generate treatment options. The ethical principle of the medical component of decision-making should be the principle of 'beneficence', where the doctor seeks to maximise patient benefit and minimise patient harm. Now 'competent adult' patients should have the ethical and legal rights to accept or reject the doctor's recommendations. Logically, according to Siegler, the informed preferences of patients must follow the doctor's recommendations. Before running another debate on whose preferences count 'most' it should be stated that our author believes that most medical decisions are reached in a non-adversarial way by combining medical indications and patient preferences!

So far so good, but ethical dilemmas may arise in clinical decision-making. One possibility is that conflicts may indeed emerge between medical indications and patient preferences. Siegler goes for the example of the Jehovah's Witness refusing a life-saving blood transfusion on religious grounds. This of course is a dramatic example, but it is clear that situations can arise where adults whose 'competence' is not in question may well refuse recommended medical treatment. A second set of possibilities is when decisions cannot be reached on the basis of either medical indications or patient preferences. Some diseases or conditions are not treatable and it could be the case that the patient is not competent to express personal wishes, for example if brain-injured.

This is where the third and fourth aspects of the clinical-ethical decision may be brought into play, namely quality of life and external considerations. It should be stressed immediately that a competent patient's own assessment of his or her quality of life comes firmly under the rubric of patient preferences that we have been contemplating. There may be a role, though, for quality-of-life judgements which are the subjective assessments by a doctor or a third party, e.g. the family, of what Siegler refers to as the 'apparent' quality of life of, say, a mentally incapacitated patient. One interesting question which arises is whether these third party subjective assessments could be provided by the sort of standardised instruments which we have been characterising in this book as health status or quality-of-life measures. It does not appear that such an approach would run counter to the clinical-ethical framework that Siegler is propounding.

By external factors are meant those considerations arising from a medical decision yielding a benefit or placing a burden on people other than the patient. This is a concept familiar to economists ('externalities') and indeed has been stressed in the medical context by Donabedian and other analysts in the notion of social quality and social utility (Donabedian *et al.*, 1982). Siegler lists the following factors: the safety of others, economic costs to society, the use of scarce medical resources (economists might well be reluctant to separate this from the previous factor!), family wishes, and the needs of medical research and teaching. The ethical questions concern how to weigh the patient's interests *vis-à-vis* those of others and society at large. As Siegler states: 'In the past external factors were not accorded great weight in resolving clinical-ethical decisions, but this is obviously changing in the current era which emphasizes cost containment and medical parsimony.' What so far has seemed a fairly innocuous or at least a not especially controversial discussion of clinical ethics begins to take on a more debatable note!

And indeed Siegler turns to the potential problems. First, clinical ethicists are criticised for over-emphasising the qualitative approach, to the detriment of the quantitative. This seems a somewhat defensive position: there is nothing in Siegler's description of the clinical-ethical framework which would appear to preclude quantification. Indeed, thinking about the interactions between this framework and health status measurement, the quantitative approach of the latter could well reinforce the clinical ethic in its quality of life and external factor categories.

Second, he refers to 'close calls'. There is no ethical dilemma if the clinical choice is an obvious one between right and wrong. But what about the right and right choices, say between telling the truth and maintaining confidentiality? Or wrong and wrong, say keeping someone alive who is in persistent vegetative state or 'causing' death by withdrawing life support? Clearly there may be a range of ethically and clinically acceptable decisions rather than a unique decision for each situation, and there may well be some completely unacceptable decisions.

Third, the assessment of patient preferences and utilities is fraught with difficulty. We saw this before in the 'whose values' discussion of Chapter 5. Siegler makes no less than nine points here. A number relate to the 'competence' of the patient. By what criteria should a patient's competence to make decisions be judged? One obvious question is whether people always mean what they say. How does the clinician know? Other issues relate to 'surrogate' judges making assessments of patients' utilities on the behalf of patients when a patient is believed to be incompetent. How competent will the judges be in these circumstances?

The material we have covered should indicate the nature of clinical ethics. For Siegler, the central research task is to develop a rich and empirical descriptive clinical ethics which is data-based and which relates to the process and outcome of clinical-ethical decisions. He feels that decision analysis in this area faces similar challenges. From the perspective of this book it would be a pity if the insights obtained from the two sets of disciplines were not to be coordinated in various ways, if not completely integrated.

CLINICAL DECISION-MAKING

It will be evident that much of the present chapter has been devoted to issues of importance for clinical decision-making, either quite directly or obliquely. David Eddy, the doctor who has been commissioned by the *Journal of the American Medical Association* to write on clinical decision-making, makes the interesting and perhaps startling claim that the changes currently under way in the methods for designing what he calls 'practice policies' represent a change in the intellectual basis of medicine (Eddy, 1990b). These policies comprise preformed recommendations issued for the purpose of influencing decisions about health interventions. Suppose such policies are not available. A health decision would involve the following: identifying the options; identifying the possible outcomes of the various options; evaluating the evidence relating options to outcomes; estimating the consequences of each option; weighing the benefits of each option against its harms and costs; taking account of logistic, economic, legal, social and personal factors; and finally choosing the 'best' option. As Eddy states: 'If every practitioner attempted to do this for every decision, the result would be either mental paralysis or chaos' (Eddy, 1990a).

Now, whilst some decisions will be made on a purely individual basis, medical practices have developed over the centuries to aid decision-making. Eddy (1990a) gives a fascinating (and lengthy) list: statements in textbooks, indications and contra-indications, drugs of choice, rules of thumb, recommended practices, essentials of diagnosis, standard practices, expert testimony, the correct answers to board examinations, and a wide variety of principles, maxims, rules, dicta, criteria and axioms.

But why and how is change taking place in practice policies? Eddy (1990a) contends that there have been 'dramatic changes in the way policies are being produced and used'. Traditionally practice policies have evolved in a decentralised sort of way which helped individual practitioners to make individual decisions. By analogy with Adam Smith's invisible hand, the medical marketplace should ensure that individual decisions result in the best practices for society, with bad practices being weeded out and good practices prevailing. Eddy sees two main changes over the last decade or so.

1. Practice policies are increasingly becoming used as active management tools: they are being designed explicitly as instruments for quality assurance, pre-certification, utilisation review, accreditation, coverage, and cost containment. The significance of all this for medical decision-making is that it opens up the possibility of external control of practice policies: the possibility that the medical profession will indeed lose its control. This means that 'physician groups must race to develop their own policies'. There are echoes of this US view in the UK, where the medical profession appears largely in favour of medical audit and where (in some contrast to the USA?) the government seems reasonably content to let medical peer review be the over-riding component, although even here there is expected to be significant managerial involvement (see Chapter 4).
2. The informal decentralised process of practice policy formation is being replaced by formal procedures shaped by committees and panels, with agendas, criteria, budgets, board approvals and dissemination plans.

Clinical decision-making appears likely under these sorts of regimes to be somewhat removed from the pure untramelled decision-making of the independent medical practitioner! No comment will be made at this stage on the desirability of these developments. In the UK the medical profession clearly views with some dismay the specification of various formal targets in general practitioners' contracts, targets on whose achievement doctors' incomes will to some extent depend. From the health status measurement point of view it is likely that wider outcome measurement will take on added significance in all the activity surrounding the shaping of practice policies. The uses of health status measurement in clinical decision-making will be further considered in Chapter 7.

PROMOTION, PREVENTION AND HEALTH STATUS MEASUREMENT

Inevitably much of the thrust of this book, this chapter being no exception, has concerned the inter-relationships between *medical* decision-making and health status measurement. 'Inevitably' because, perhaps inappropriately from an overall health and welfare standpoint, the medical care area commands substantial resources in most countries, with the concomitant substantial interest in matters medical. At times we have used the term 'health intervention' to indicate that there are broader factors at work than the purely medical in contributing to people's health, welfare and happiness. Let us then, however briefly, try to redress the balance a little.

Whilst the terms are not necessarily interchangeable, promotion and prevention have the same essential aim in mind, namely good health for all. Maintaining good health and avoiding premature death are the key outcomes. Health status measurement ought to have its part to play in judging and assessing/evaluating health promotion and prevention schemes, since it is explicitly concerned with those entities which may enable judgements to be made about the usefulness or otherwise of health interventions of all kinds. We will focus on prevention, but it should be evident that a similar analysis can be applied to promotion.

Analysis of prevention is usually divided into three categories: primary, secondary and tertiary (Buchan *et al.*, 1990). Primary prevention aims to prevent the onset or reduce the incidence of disease, disability or handicap, where incidence refers to the number of new cases of the disease or condition occurring in a defined population over a specified time period. Strategies here cover a wide range of possibilities: genetic counselling, immunisation, anti-smoking campaigns, water fluoridation, and motorway crash barriers, for example. Secondary prevention is about reducing the prevalence or burden of disease, that is the proportion of people with a given disease or condition in a given population at a specified point in time. By prevention it may be possible to shorten the duration of disease through early diagnosis and treatment. Many screening programmes fall into this category, although some may be operative at the primary stage if they are aimed at detecting the risk factors for disease. Tertiary prevention aims to reduce the complications of disease once it has occurred and to minimise long-term disability if possible.

Preventive measures can be aimed at people thought or judged to be at high risk, or at entire communities. Clearly there is a substantial role for 'social' decision-making here, since the prevention of infectious diseases has important 'spillover' effects: prevention of the disease in one person reduces the chances of other people catching the disease. In enhancing or preserving health status we may of course be promoting the effectiveness of the use of a community's resources. And of course if we combine the measurement of health status with the economic aspects of resource use, using an evaluative approach such as cost-utility analysis, we ought to be promoting efficiency as well.

A significant problem is that the outcome of preventive measures has to be assessed in populations, whereas the outcomes of therapeutic actions more obviously concern individuals (Black, 1989). 'It may follow that to increase relative expenditure on preventive measures, as is so often advocated, has to a certain extent to be a matter of faith, as with some dietary measures, or justified by retrospective analysis of the type that revealed the link between smoking and lung cancer.'

CONCLUSION

This chapter has covered a wide range of issues under the broad rubric of decision-making, with perhaps as much emphasis on the principles involved as the practice. In the final chapter an attempt will be made to look within a broad framework at decision-taking and to consider the significance of health status measurement in the context of the rapid changes taking place in the health sector, changes not confined to any particular country's health system.

CHAPTER 7

Trends and Issues

It is tempting to start this concluding chapter with the observation that health status measurement is an idea whose time has come. This would be to do an injustice to the likes of Graunt, Petty, Farr, Nightingale and Codman, whose concerns with the measurement of health and the assessment of the outcomes of medical procedures span the centuries. It would also be misleading if the impression were to be given that medical and other health personnel have not hitherto been concerned in various ways with the outcomes of their efforts. Nor would one want to imply that health status measurement is the latest fad or fashion, destined to be discarded or ignored when the next fashion comes along. Be that as it may, there is no doubt that the volume of work in health status and health-related quality of life measurement has expanded to such an extent in recent years that phrases such as 'explosion of interest' have been used to characterise developments in these areas. This explosion has not just been in evidence in the 'professional' literature: newspapers and magazines regularly contain references to such concepts as the QALY. Conferences on outcome measurement proceed apace, both for health status researchers and analysts, and for health service personnel who may be expected to become involved in such measurement.

One of the reasons for these developments is what has been perceived to be the need for the *systematic* measurement and assessment of groups of patients/clients, with evaluation and policy issues in mind. More detailed reasons for these developments were outlined in Chapter 1. Subsequent chapters have explored the methodology and 'mechanics' of measurement. We have also dealt in some detail in our coverage of this material with various major issues connected with health status and quality of life measurement.

We have seen how complex are many of the issues and what a broad range of activity and interests comprise this area of endeavour. Thus some selectivity is required for this final chapter in order to keep matters manageable. First, some general observations about a number of trends in health status measurement will be presented and then the uses to which health status and quality of life measurement are being (or could be) put are examined. A number of topics which have been of continuing interest to analysts will then be contemplated: theoretical foundations and conceptual focus, measurement over time, psychometrics and scaling, and whose values?

An attempt will be made to answer a number of questions. How far are the health status measurement techniques being used for evaluative purposes?

Are the measures actually being used in decision-making? What trends can be discerned in the application of such measurement? What substantive concerns have been exercising health measurement analysts? At various stages in the book there has been commentary on matters relevant for answers to these questions. This chapter expands upon this commentary.

SOME TRENDS IN HEALTH STATUS MEASUREMENT

Let us start with a few general observations on a number of trends in health status measurement. First, it could be argued that there is an increasing coherence in the terminology being used. This may seem surprising, given the substantial increase in the number of people and groups working in the area. On the other hand, presumably partly *because* of this increase, there have been determined efforts by some analysts to attempt to 'get a grip' on the way matters are developing and to pronounce on methodology and terminology, often in the context of major conferences or through the medium of special issues of journals. In addition articles and textbooks are appearing with more frequency which explain to potential users or developers of health status measures how to go about their tasks. This has led to a recognisable and reasonably standardised vocabulary. It would be wise not to overstress this judgement, though. The debate on what constitutes 'quality', reported in Chapter 4, is as good an example as any that caution is in order! We shall also consider shortly some of the issues that continue to be raised in the matters of theoretical foundations and conceptual focus.

Second, the various established measures or instruments are becoming more widely disseminated and used. This could be regarded as a helpful development — it suggests that expertise already developed is being put to use, leaving less inclination for newcomers to 'reinvent the wheel'. Of course this presupposes that the right wheel(s) is or are now available!

A very useful bibliography (Spilker *et al.*, 1990) comprising 578 references can be used to indicate the 'spread' of health status and quality-of-life measurement. The authors provide a helpful set of classifications of the measures referenced. First they classify the papers by instruments. The most 'popular' numerically are shown in Table 7.1. The instruments tabulated clearly cover the gamut of health status measures outlined in Chapter 2.

Second, Spilker's bibliography provides a listing of the papers referenced by 'therapeutic category'. The classification is by 23 categories, which indicates the wide range of therapeutic areas now covered by the measures. 'Popular' categories comprise oncology (108 papers), cardiovascular disease (103), mental health (65), surgery (60), rheumatological disease (53), nervous system diseases (45), and geriatrics (35). The last number would certainly underestimate the geriatric health status work that has been undertaken. The list still remains suggestive, however, of the concern for health status

Table 7.1 Frequency of usage of measurement instruments

Katz ADL (used in 20 papers)
American Rheumatological Association Functional Classification (10)
Arthritis Impact Measurement Scale (22)
Bradburn Psychological Well-Being or Affect Balance Scale (13)
Functional Status Index (10)
Health Assessment Questionnaire (13)
Karnofsky Performance Status Scale (39)
Life Satisfaction Index (18)
LASA Scale (16)
McGill Pain Questionnaire (14)
McMaster Health Index Questionnaire (13)
Minnesota Multiple Personality Inventory (17)
New York Heart Association Classification (13)
Nottingham Health Profile (12)
Profile of Mood States (15)
Psychological Adjustment to Illness Scale (10)
Spitzer Q-L Index (18)
Quality Adjusted Life-Years (12)
Rand Health Insurance Study Measures (18)
Sickness Impact Profile (49)

Source: Calculated from Spilker et al., 1990.

and quality-of-life assessment in these major therapeutic areas. The general interest in the issues surrounding health status and quality-of-life measurement is confirmed by the relatively large number of papers (99) the authors classify in the category 'quality of life: measurement issues and general discussion'.

Finally the authors list the instruments themselves by therapeutic category: this classification indicates quite clearly again the spread of the instruments across different diseases and conditions, and in addition the extraordinary variety of instruments used within these categories. On the latter the cardiovascular diseases category has been subject to as many as 81 measures. Other 'scores' are 47 in geriatrics, 61 for mental health, 92 in oncology, and 39 in rheumatology.

Unfortunately Spilker's work is not fully comprehensive! A comparison with the present author's own, slightly later, survey containing 730 references shows just 148 references common to the two surveys (Brooks, 1991). Meanwhile Gerrard (1991) has reviewed cost-utility analysis papers making use of QALYs. She found 51 studies using this approach for the period 1980-90.

Some evidence of geographical coverage is given in her paper. Although the majority of papers were from the US, the UK and Canada, the other countries featured were Australia, Denmark, Finland, France, Germany, Italy, The Netherlands, New Zealand, Norway, Spain, and also the West Africa region.

USES OF HEALTH STATUS AND QUALITY-OF-LIFE MEASURES

A number of potential uses for quality-of-life measurement have been suggested – as good a list as any is that of Fletcher (1993): *(i)* population, *(ii)* specific groups, *(iii)* clinical practice, *(iv)* evaluation of health services or treatments, *(v)* resource allocation.

Population

It ought in principle to be possible to have descriptive measures of health status and quality of life for the population as a whole, for example as part of the General Household Survey in the UK. Health questions have been asked in this survey, so why not incorporate health-related quality-of-life variables so that changes over time can be observed and perhaps targets set? This would appear to conform with the more general 'social indicator' movement for the categorisation of national performance. With respect to the sort of measures with which we have been dealing in this book, Fletcher suggests that health profiles may have a role to play, possibly in their short form versions. More controversially, perhaps, would be the use of the single score, aggregate version of the generic instruments in this population context. If the determination of 'social preferences' can be agreed upon for a particular country, then why not?!

Specific Groups

It will be evident from the outline of the spread of the instruments given above that health status and quality of life measurement is now being widely employed in the context of particular patient groups and conditions. There are plenty of examples available of what was described in Chapter 3 as 'nominal' measurement. Health status measures can evidently be used for descriptive purposes, for sorting and classifying and categorising such groups.

As Fletcher points out, such 'descriptive data can be used to identify areas where future interventions or treatments can be targeted'. Moving from helpful description to the use of such data for medical audit purposes, and perhaps even further to act as an aid in purchasing decisions, is more problematic, as Fletcher avers.

Clinical Practice

Again, there is no doubting the increased interest in the application of health status measurement in clinical practice. In the USA the third in the series of big conferences (held this time in Washington) entitled 'Advances in Health Status Assessment' was largely devoted to the issues involved in this potential area of application (Lohr, 1992). In terms of trends and change the choice of this theme indicates the increased interest in moving health status measurement out of the research arena and into everyday clinical practice.

Many of the matters raised at the conference had been addressed in earlier literature so that for a detailed look at the use of health status measurement in clinical practice we can turn to a very interesting and helpful paper by Nelson and Berwick (1989). Initially these authors point out that few clinicians have adopted health status measurement as a routine component of their practices. In general, they suggest, the best measurement tools have been developed for research use rather than for clinical practice. We considered Berwick's views on this matter in Chapter 4. But the authors do feel that the newer tools are, in principle, 'friendlier to the potential practitioner-user'. They tabulate 21 instruments that may be suited for direct clinical use, their criteria for selection to the list being: *(i)* relevance of content to office-based practice, *(ii)* length, *(iii)* potential for self-administration by the patient, *(iv)* validity and reliability, and *(v)* ease of scoring and interpretation. These criteria of practicality, validity and reliability were of course considered earlier in Chapter 3. The 21 instruments comprise 5 physical function measures, 6 mental health measures, 4 multidimensional measures, and 6 'other health related measures'. Examples include the Katz ADL scale, the PULSES profile, the General Health Questionnaire, the Mental Health Inventory, the COOP charts, the Nottingham Health Profile, the Spitzer Quality of Life Index and the Arthritis Impact Measurement Scales.

The authors then go on to ask if formal measures of health status make a difference. Their answer is 'yes' for the *geriatric* area with evidence sparse for other areas, in particular primary care. They cite a review by Rubenstein (1987), who found evidence supporting the impact of geriatric functional assessment on patient outcomes in areas such as diagnostic accuracy, patterns of medication, and functional and emotional health status. Further citations suggest that:

1. There are many examples of programmes which have documented multiple benefits of comprehensive assessment of frail elderly patients.
2. Comprehensive geriatric assessment and consultation services in hospital settings have produced improvements in the fit between continuing care plans and patients' functional needs.
3. Various home visiting randomised trials coupled with functional assessment have shown favourable effects.

On *primary care* they are able to cite only a handful of studies using the GHQ, the FSQ, and the COOP charts. Nevertheless, interest in the primary care applications of health-related quality of life is without doubt on the increase, with such recent texts as Wilkin *et al.* (1992) and Stewart *et al.* (1992) taking primary care as their main focus.

For other examples of applications we can turn to Aaronson *et al.* (1991) who, in reviewing quality-of-life measurement in oncology, state that changes in clinical practice have occurred on the basis of quality-of-life findings in the administration of central nervous system radiation for children with acute lymphocytic leukaemia, the surgical development of early breast cancer, and the treatment of soft tissue sarcoma.

Nelson and Berwick (1989) then discuss the barriers to the clinical use of formal health status measurement. Three types of barriers are identified. First, doctors may lack confidence in the validity of the information provided by the measures. Second, even if the doctors accept the validity of the measures, they may be doubtful if such measures can help the patient. They suggest that the scarcity of controlled trials using health status measures reported in the literature is a serious flaw in this regard. Third, health status measurement may raise anxiety and therefore resistance in doctors already feeling overwhelmed by their workloads. However, they point out, this may just reflect resistance to questionnaires in general, not health status measurement in particular.

To circumvent these barriers the authors 'suspect that ease of administration (preferably by patients, perhaps during waiting room time), ease of scoring, and simplicity of interpretation all will be non-negotiable requirements for any instrument with a chance of achieving widespread use in stressed office settings'. This is supported by Aaronson *et al.* (1991): 'If we hope to incorporate quality of life considerations into clinical decision-making, we will need to develop short, practical, and simple tools that can be used in clinical practice by patients and their physicians.' Nelson and Berwick consider that recent work on short-form instruments holds considerable potential in that it seems that a great deal of information can still be preserved using these shorter measures. In a similar vein Cox *et al.* (1992), in a detailed article concerned about the methods used in quality-of-life measurement, which pointed to such problems as instruments being developed in one context being applied in studies with different objectives, commend simplicity in quality-of-life measurement. Among their recommendations are: (*i*) 'simplicity should be the keynote wherever possible (whether with respect to design, analysis or presentation); (*ii*) presentation of results of QOL assessments should, as well as being as simple as possible, facilitate their use in treatment decisions for individual patients, and interpretation of the clinical significance of effects'.

These attempts to generate instruments serving 'practical' purposes clearly represent an important strand of current health status and quality-of-life work.

The Nelson and Berwick article concludes in an interesting fashion with a discussion of the potential of health status measurement. Among the possible benefits are:

1. Enhanced doctor–patient communication – 'opening the door for important discussions, reluctant disclosure and areas of concern'.
2. Possible reductions in the amount of time spent in gathering needed information from patients, perhaps whilst patients are waiting to see the doctor, and where the use of ancillary staff in this endeavour may increase their productivity, sense of professionalism and job satisfaction.
3. Properly constructed instruments could be enjoyable for the patient to employ.
4. Health status measurement could contribute to better disease-specific outcomes, could permit earlier detection of illnesses, could help towards better treatment planning, may allow for more precisely timed alterations in therapeutic plans, and may provide useful and encouraging feedback to patients in convalescence.
5. Routine use of well-established health measurement tools 'would offer the research community much richer information on the trajectory of function for specific diseases and specific populations, thereby offering better opportunities for wiser allocation of resources and more appropriate allocation of efforts in research and program development'.

This is an upbeat litany, to say the least! Their article, however, is far from uncritical in its consideration of health status measurement, so their views on its potential are well taken. It should be evident from this discussion that unless there are incentives for the 'players' involved to use health status measures, then mere exhortation of the virtues and potential of such measurement will not suffice. The incentives do not have to be monetary, although a number of comments at the Washington conference placed some stress on this aspect: 'the ideal instrument needs to be profitable if it is going to be accepted in most clinical situations' (Tuteur, 1992); 'we should never underestimate the perverse purposes to which the third-party-payer system component of the health care system might put these instruments' (Nutting, in Bergner et al., 1992); 'I think you cannot overestimate the willingness of people, physicians and organisations to ask questions if they think it is going to make more money' (Goldberg et al., 1992).

Lest it be felt that this question of incentives is confined to the sort of health financing arrangements existing in the USA, consider the possibilities in the mainly publicly financed system in the UK, which is becoming subject to market procedures through the split between purchasers and providers, and through an elaborate system of contracts between the 'players' in the system. Suppose purchasers, in attempting to achieve 'value for money', decide that measures of health status and quality of life are required outcome indicators, as can be anticipated when serious consideration comes to be given to outcome measures in addition to the more easily handled cost-per-unit-of-service type of assessment of health sector activity. It can be predicted that it would not take too long for providers to engage in such measurement, since of course finance flows would become more dependent upon the recommended outcome measurement.

Perhaps we should treat the question of incentives as a topic for discussion in its own right, rather than subsume it in the present context of clinical practice. There is little doubt that action by individuals and organisations is crucially influenced by incentive structures. This evidently applies, as we shall now observe, to the next area of application, that of pharmaceuticals.

Pharmaceuticals

Turning from clinical practice, let us consider developments in the applications of health status and quality-of-life measurement to the pharmaceutical arena. The first point to be made is that the inclusion of such measurement in clinical trials can provide additional outcomes for use in economic evaluation such as cost-effectiveness analysis and cost-utility analysis. Indeed, as we have seen, measures such as the QALY may constitute *the* relevant outcome measure.

How is the pharmaceutical industry reacting to modern measurement methods? Writing in the US context, Revicki (1990) points to a survey sponsored by the Institute of Medicine which found that almost two-thirds of responding pharmaceutical companies indicated that they are using quality-of-life measures in clinical trials. Further, he states that the findings from quality-of-life studies are being used in the marketing of different drugs, especially where there are competing therapies.

In the USA also the National Institutes of Health have incorporated quality-of-life assessments in large-scale clinical trials of treatments for cardiovascular disease, insulin dependent diabetes mellitus, and cancer. Revicki further expects the Food and Drug Administration (FDA) to make use of such assessments in the FDA approval process as measurement techniques improve.

As Revicki points out, a drug can be clinically efficaceous but have negative quality-of-life consequences.

> In a competitive environment, with a number of alternative therapies, demonstrated quality of life outcomes may make the difference between the success or failure of a new product. There is a tremendous waste of resources due to noncompliance, including additional and unnecessary diagnostic testing and decreased efficacy of the treatment which often lead to increased use of health services.

He is strongly in favour of the addition of quality-of-life measures to clinical trials, particularly as such additions should only increase costs minimally. He pens a nice succinct list of the situations for which quality-of-life measurement is most useful, namely: where there are slight differences in survival between alternative therapies under comparison; where there are several equally effective therapies for a specific medical condition; where the therapy is effective in decreasing mortality, but is toxic, leading to additional morbidity; where the therapy is lifelong, the disease complication rate is low, and patients are asymptomatic or have mild symptoms.

The volume of work in the economic evaluation of drugs has increased substantially in recent years. One indication has been the establishment in 1992 of a new journal (*Pharmacoeconomics*) devoted to the inter-relationship between economics and pharmaceuticals.

In a review of methods for assessing the effects of drug therapy on quality of life Ganz (1990) pointed out that, apart from a few studies, 'assessments of quality of life have often been tacked on as an afterthought to clinical studies evaluating drug therapy'. It is likely that matters have been changing in this regard recently as the volume of work increases. Two studies which did incorporate health status measurement within their original designs are those of Croog et al. (1986) and Bombardier et al. (1986). Croog's study was a multi-centre, randomised, double-blind clinical trial, in which men with mild to moderate hypertension were evaluated for the effects of captopril, methyldopa and propranolol on quality of life and control of blood pressure. It was observed that different hypertensive medications do vary in their impact on various aspects of quality of life.

The auranofin trial was a randomised, double-blind, multi-centre trial which compared auranofin with placebo in patients with rheumatoid arthritis (Bombardier, et al., 1986). The trial showed that auranofin therapy was superior to placebo using standard clinical measures, a finding which was largely confirmed using a battery of health status measures. This battery included examples of most of the categories of health status instruments we have been dealing with in this book. Examples include the Keitel Assessment, the Health Assessment Questionnaire, the Quality of Well-Being Questionnaire, the Patient Utility Measurement Set, a Standard Gamble questionnaire and a Willingness-to-Pay questionnaire.

All this activity has not gone without critical comment. Perhaps partly because of the marketing potential within a competitive environment, drug companies have been willing to fund major measurement studies, especially within the context of clinical trials. This provides a good example of the incentive point made in the previous section. But, as Fletcher (1993) points out: 'More results are published showing benefits in quality of life for the sponsor's drug than might seem reasonable.' This may result, she states, from the strategy of using a poor comparator drug; and it is 'likely that many trials with equivalent or negative results do not get further than company files'. Revicki *et al.* (1992) also point to (*i*) 'the selection of comparative medical treatments that bias the study in favour of the new treatment', and (*ii*) 'selection of health-related quality of life assessment instruments which do not measure adverse effects of the drugs under study'. The methodological requirements for measurement that have been treated in this book undoubtedly apply *a fortiori* to drug evaluation, involving as this does important ethical issues as well the substantial deployment of resources. Apart from the marketing aspect, many drug companies have for defensive reasons, with governments requiring or likely to require that new drugs be shown to be cost-effective, incorporated economic appraisal into clinical trials, as we have observed. This tendency may be reinforced in the UK context, for example, by the purchasers of health care within the new market framework insisting on cost-effectiveness and 'value for money' in drug usage.

Fletcher (1993) advocates that all trials, whatever their phase of development, should be registered with an independent agency, such as the UK Clearing House for Information on the Assessment of Health Outcomes. There seems no reason why this should not also apply to new medical technology. Such a requirement may help to improve the evaluation of new treatments, not least by reducing the possibilities of biased procedures since as a result more independent assessment could be incorporated into evaluation.

Resource Allocation

Since this book has been concerned from the outset with the contemplation of outcome measurement within an economic framework, it is clearly very important to review the place of health status and health-related quality-of-life measurement in the context of resource allocation. To do this we must return to the QALY notion, as this is often explicitly listed as *the* outcome measure in cost-utility analysis.

QALYS

For a concept that only started on its (formal) life in the mid-1970s, the literature on QALYs has become very extensive, reflecting both the increasing use of QALY measures for empirical work and the critiques and criticism that have emerged in consequence. The debate on QALYs has, a little surprisingly to the present author, often polarised into economists versus 'the critics'. Some reasons for this were put forward in an earlier publication (Brooks, 1991): perhaps it is because economists are explicit about their search for, and advocacy of, evaluative methods for use in resource allocation; or perhaps the appearance of cost/QALY league tables, with their explicit linking of costs to QALY outcome measures, and explicit ranking of health and medical procedures and interventions, acts as a provocation. It should be stated at the outset, however, that there is nothing inherently 'economic' about the QALY as an outcome measure and to attribute the development of QALYs solely to economists would be very misleading and would ignore the important and substantial efforts of researchers and analysts from other disciplines. It is also the case that criticism of the concept and its development has emerged from economists, a good example being the detailed paper of Loomes and McKenzie (1989).

There is no intention to review the debate concerning QALYs in full: we shall simply select a number of issues to help give the flavour of the arguments.

A QALY measure encompasses two dimensions: quantity – usually comprising life-expectancy or life-years, and quality – employing a set of weights to quality-adjust these life-years. It will not come as a surprise to learn that considerable controversy surrounds the nature of the weighting used in this quality adjustment. Once life-years have been adjusted, the 'productivity' of a medical or health intervention can be defined as the difference over a period of time between expected QALYs with the intervention and without it.

The convenience or significance of the QALY concept is that it provides 'a common denominator with respect to which the consequences of programs with diverse objectives and clinical endpoints may be compared' (Weinstein, 1988). Note the general nature of the term 'intervention': it is not just medical care that can be assessed in QALY terms. Indeed such interventions as 'General Practitioner advice to give up smoking' can be observed in the published league tables (see Table 7.2). Having such a common denominator holds out the prospect, according to its advocates, of aiding rational decision-making including, perhaps even especially, at the societal level.

One set of criticisms surrounds the nature and construction of the QALY measure itself, with particular reference to the weighting procedures. It should be evident within the context of this book that such measurement issues are not specific to the QALY concept. In illustrating the development of formal and explicit health status measures in previous chapters we have observed many of the complexities of such formal measurement.

Two examples of this type of criticism are:

1. The mortality and morbidity data on which QALY calculations are based are not sufficiently precise – this is clearly not specific to QALY measurement and simply means that if this is the case then suitable efforts should be devoted to generating and retrieving the appropriate data, whether for QALYs or for other uses.
2. Different scaling methods (category scaling, the standard gamble, etc.) could produce different weights for quality adjustment when measuring the same phenomenon. This point is well taken, but would only mean the abandonment specifically of the QALY concept if it was judged to be

Table 7.2 Quality adjusted life-year (QALY) of competing therapies: some tentative estimates

	Cost/QALY (£ Aug 1990)
Cholesterol testing and diet therapy only (all adults, aged 40–69)	220
Neurosurgical intervention for head injury	240
GP advice to stop smoking	270
Neurosurgical intervention for subarachnoid haemorrhage	490
Anti-hypertensive therapy to prevent stroke (ages 45–64)	940
Pacemaker implantation	1 100
Hip replacement	1 140
Valve replacement for aortic stenosis	1 180
Cholesterol testing and treatment	1 480
Coronary artery bypass graft (CABG) (left main vessel disease, severe angina)	2 090
Kidney transplant	4 710
Breast cancer screening	5 780
Heart transplantation	7 840
Cholesterol testing and treatment (incrementally) of all adults 25–39 years	14 150
Home haemodialysis	17 260
CABG (1 vessel disease, moderate angina)	18 830
Continuous ambulatory peritoneal dialysis	19 870
Hospital haemodialysis	21 970
Erythropoietin treatment for anaemia in dialysis patients (assuming a 10% reduction in mortality)	54 380
Neurosurgical intervention for malignant intracranial tumours	107 780
Erythropoietin treatment for anaemia in dialysis (assuming no increase in survival)	126 290

Source: Maynard, 1991.

fundamentally flawed for this reason. At this stage of the development of the QALY and of health status measurement more generally it would appear unduly harsh to argue this, although some analysts would gladly have the QALY approach abandoned forthwith!

Another set of criticisms could be taken independently, and essentially relates to the usefulness or otherwise of the QALY approach in evaluation and decision-making, although 'fundamentals' could be at issue, as we shall note. A substantial body of this criticism surrounds cost/QALY league tables, to which we now turn. One key criticism can be succinctly put: cost/QALY league tables are dangerous because they suggest quick and easy solutions to the decision-maker. Presumably the decision-maker in this context could be the politician or administrator making decisions about the allocation of funds across major programmes, i.e. at some 'over-arching' (societal) level, or, at 'lower' levels, administrators and/or clinicians deciding upon the disbursement of given budgets under their control or influence, say at the individual hospital level. The 'quick-and-easy' argument is that league tables might lead to less thought by decision-makers about the difficulty and complexity of health care choices, thus perhaps proving counter-productive. This argument is a familiar one, pointing as it does to the temptation or proclivity for people – analysts, researchers, advisers, decision-makers – to use available techniques as substitutes for thought, creative appraisal and careful policy determination. QALY critics arguing in this vein suggest that the approach is likely to obscure the truth about health and health valuations rather than reveal it, because people become enamoured of the simple calculus whose results are represented in the league tables.

One answer given to this criticism is that the procedure adopted in QALY construction *is* explicit about the value judgements being made concerning health status, and if critics are unhappy with the procedure (rather than the principle) then they can always seek to improve the QALY approach by modifying it in ways that they deem appropriate.

Another criticism is that it is unwise to make broad comparisons across widely different medical fields. Some analysts have urged therefore that QALYs be largely calculated for programme-specific decisions (Donaldson *et al.*, 1988). This issue about the 'level' at which QALYs can or should be applied remains largely unresolved.

A further issue is the argument that strict application of cost/QALY league tables would imply that those whose treatment has a high cost/QALY would receive no care. Priority rankings of the sort developed in the Oregon experiment are of interest in this context. This exercise explicitly ranked a variety of treatments on cost-effectiveness grounds, where the effectiveness was measured in the form of the expected net benefit from each treatment, based upon the Bush Quality of Well-Being approach, essentially a form of QALY. For example dental caps were estimated to give an average quality-of-life improvement of about 8 per cent over non-treatment, whereas an appendectomy was expected to result in a 97 per cent improvement. But, as Hadorn (1991) points out:

> These reasonable estimates did not translate into reasonable (relative) priority ratings, however. Although both surgical procedures for appendectomy and ectopic pregnancy were correctly estimated to entail a far higher level and duration of benefit than either of the two minor treatments, [tooth capping and splints for temporomandibular joint disease] the relatively high costs of surgery effectively neutralised these outcome considerations, producing nearly identical priority ratings for all four treatments.

Hadorn argues that ranking by cost-effectiveness in this way is not appropriate. A two-stage procedure he advocates was then adopted: set priorities first on the basis of net expected health benefit, then determine the degree of benefit required before services are deemed necessary, for example how close to the top of the list generated (in the first stage) a treatment would need to be for coverage to be provided under Medicaid. In other words costs (and resource availability) are not linked to outcomes at the outset, but *after* prioritisation by health benefit, a procedure criticised by Maynard (1993). This two-stage approach still does not, it is clear, rule out the use of QALYs, it simply affects the way they might be used in resource allocation.

In August 1992 the federal government denied approval for the latest version of Oregon's proposal (Power, 1992), arguing that 'the method used to create the prioritised list, which included applying public estimates of the quality of life associated with various health states, violated the Americans With Disabilities Act.' However, in March 1993, the Clinton administration approved the latest version of Oregon's plan. This action would seem to indicate that the formal setting of priorities *is* capable of meeting political approval. Whether QALYs should be used in resource allocation remains at issue, though.

Objections to the use of QALY league tables for resource allocation purposes can also be taken as part of the attack on QALYs which argues that the approach is not explicitly concerned with equity or justice in the distribution of health care resources. More generally it should be reported that a substantial strand of the QALY debate has concerned moral principles, fairness and justice, with commentators rejecting QALYs on the basis of a variety of ethical principles (see Harris, 1987; Broome, 1988; Kawachi, 1989; Williams, 1988, for the flavour of this debate). The most common 'ethical' line taken by QALY supporters is to treat a QALY as 'worth' the same to every individual. QALYs may ultimately founder on moral/ethical principles, but the concept seems unlikely to be swept under the carpet just yet.

A SELECTION OF ISSUES

We turn now from the potential uses of health status measures to a number of issues which have been exercising the minds of many of the analysts and researchers involved in outcome measurement. These issues recur at conferences and in the literature so that it would be remiss in any review of the changing 'state of the art' not to pinpoint the more important. What constitutes the 'most important' must essentially come down to a personal choice when there is such a rich amount of material available. The selection is as follows: theoretical foundations, dynamics, psychometrics and scaling, and whose values?

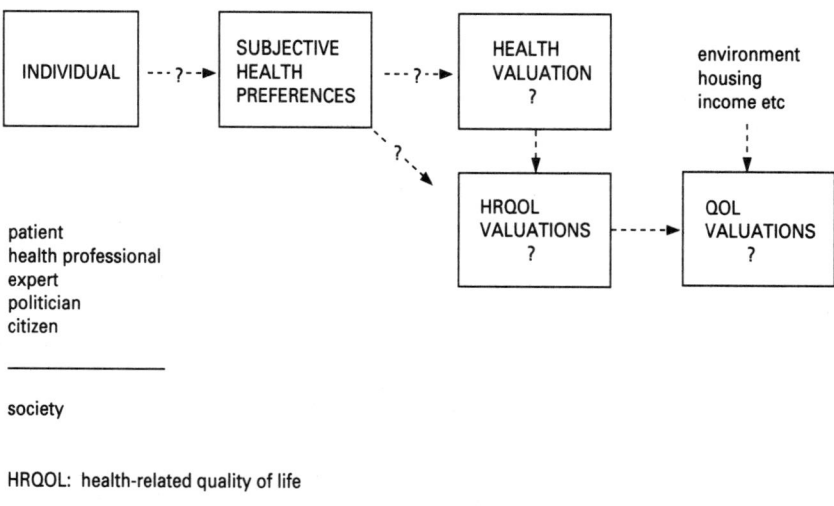

Figure 7.1 A conceptual scheme for valuation in health

Theoretical Foundations

Consider Figure 7.1, which is a somewhat simplified depiction of the complex area with which we have been concerned. Pictured therein is a 'chain' linking the individual to quality-of-life valuations. Question marks are positioned for most of the links in the chain and for the valuations themselves. Much of this book has been concerned in one way or another with these valuations, but a number of analysts (for example Veit and Ware, 1982; Mor and Guadagnoli, 1988; and Angel and Gronfein, 1988) have been keen to explore the underlying theoretical foundations of all this activity, or, perhaps more accurately, the *lack of* adequate exploration of the 'cognitive processes' which (under)pin the links in the chain.

What is required, according to such analysts, is the development of an underlying theory which would enable subjective causal hypotheses to be tested. How do people form their preferences? How do their underlying (subjective) beliefs translate into health valuations and health-related quality of life valuations? If people are to be asked to scale or rate health states then, it is argued, this must be done as a test of some hypothesis concerning the process by which valuations are accomplished. Clearly context is important: health states and quality of life are likely to be influenced by such matters as disease progression and duration, life stage and, for want of a better 'catch all' word, the 'culture' within which we operate. These elements all shape the cognitive processes which people bring to bear in the health area.

McDowell and Newell (1987) discuss the conceptual bases for health measurements. In their view there are two basic approaches: the empirical and the theoretical. The empirical approach is typically used when the measurement has some practical purpose, such as when to discharge a patient home following a rehabilitation programme. Statistical procedures are used based on correlation methods to select the appropriate questions to be used in an instrument, namely those that will best predict outcomes. This approach, however, does not help in understanding *why* these questions are appropriate since they may not be grounded in any particular theory (of rehabilitation, say). The alternative approach, favoured by McDowell and Newell, is 'to choose questions considered relevant from the standpoint of a particular theory of health'. If accomplished for each measure this will help in the determination of the validity of the measure. The authors' text proceeds to assess the conceptual bases of all the measures they review: this produces mixed results on how well founded, conceptually, are the various instruments.

Much work evidently remains to be done on the theoretical foundations of health status measurement. Ware (see Mosteller *et al.*, 1989) has suggested:

> The testing of models of health transitions deserves a high priority in future research. This research should have many agendas including studies of treatment and general health outcomes; linkages between changes in clinical measures of disease severity and general health concepts; and social, psychological, and other health factors that might account for variations in patient outcomes.

'Position' papers continue to appear in the literature, for example Cox *et al.* (1992) and Fitzpatrick (1993), so it is unlikely that any lessening of concern for the conceptual foundations of health status and quality-of-life measurement will occur: we can expect the 'keepers of the theoretical conscience' to remind us periodically to justify our analytical approaches!

Dynamics

In Ware's comment just above, the word 'transitions' can be observed. This provides a cue for our next topic, that of change over time. Few health status analysts would claim that the measurement accomplished to date contains much work of a truly dynamic nature. Ironically, given the volume of work undertaken since then, some of the early work on health indexes was much concerned with transition probabilities between health states. Most of the measures can, in principle, be used to assess change over time. Thus patients can be scored on health status before and after treatment to consider the outcome of treatment: indeed, this is often the whole point of the exercise. Further, the scaling method can either be specifically adapted to allow for time judgements: e.g., suggesting to raters that a particular health state will last for a specified period of time so that this may influence their valuations; or the scaling method may explicitly apply to time judgements as in the time trade-off approach. A number of issues in the assessment of quality-of-life changes over time have recently been reviewed by Fitzpatrick (1993).

Time preference and the associated discounting procedures have received some recent attention with analysts wrestling with the problem of the comparability of health state and quality-of-life valuations over time (Lipscomb, 1989). The issue of the discounting of health benefits, and specifically of QALYs, has produced a fierce debate which perhaps deserves a section all to itself (Krahn and Gafni, 1992; Clyne and Tolley, 1992). We are not talking here about the mere squabbling of the protagonists over some arcane point: if, for example, QALYs are to be discounted then the empirical impact on the evaluation of health interventions may be very significant.

Further difficulties and questions remain. One complex matter is that of prognosis: the ability to predict the future course of a disease or condition. We evidently live in an uncertain, not to say risky, world and the medical aspects of our world may be more uncertain than most. Health status measurement over time could presumably depend on the skilful application of prognostic information. But would this be dynamic? And what of the risks involved of falling into the *post hoc, ergo propter hoc* fallacy, a form of the hasty generalisation fallacy where it is inferred that because one event followed another – say cure followed treatment – this event must be the effect of the other?

Some empirical work on the dynamic aspects of health status measurement has been undertaken. A very interesting example is worth considering in a little detail to indicate the possibilities of dynamic measurement. Verbrugge and Balaban (1989) suggest: 'one's sense of well-being, physical symptoms from a chronic condition, and disability from it are dynamic. They fluctuate over time in response to disease activity and to medical and personal interventions.' These authors are concerned with 'real-world dynamics' in older populations. They studied 165 persons aged 55 and over who were followed for a minimum of one year after being in hospital for a chronic condition. Amongst the measures used were ADL measures and the Bush Index of Well-Being, and respondents kept health diaries continuously for a year, rating their health and activity each day. A number of interesting themes emerged from the time profiles plotted by the authors:

1. People tend to a basic mode for the diary period – either persistently stable or moderately/highly dynamic, with the degree of dynamics differing greatly across respondents.
2. Large declines in health or activity tend to be abrupt whilst sizeable

improvements are typically gradual over several weeks or months.
3. Shifts are more frequent in health than in activity. Activity changes occur in close association with health changes, usually on the same day.
4. On the majority of diary days people feel the 'same as usual'. Long-term declines or improvements in health status are eventually normalised with the criteria for 'usual' being revised accordingly.
5. Severe chronic conditions force people to change their activities.
6. Hospitalisation almost always gives a boost to well-being and activity.

These results indicate the sort of insights that may be gained from the development of a more explicitly dynamic approach to health status measurement. Clearly this approach is itself time-consuming and thus likely to be costly! It does, however, address some fundamental questions concerning the role of health status measurement in assessing health interventions, so it would be disappointing if the measurement 'industry' did not take a lead from this sort of approach. A possible way of addressing the cost issue would be for the routine use of health status measures in, say, clinical practice, so that monitoring over time could take place, which would take us back to the matters aired in an earlier section of this chapter.

Psychometrics and Scaling

These topics taken together constitute a very significant portion of the continuing concerns of health-related quality-of-life analysts. For that reason we discuss these topics again in this final chapter. An assortment of issues has already been dealt with in previous chapters so we will simply raise the more contentious and therefore those more likely to remain to the fore. We are concerned here *inter alia* with: establishing the properties of selected measures, especially their reliability and responsiveness; the meaning of validity for particular purposes; the comparison of different scaling methods (and the validity and reliability of these methods themselves).

Perhaps the least contentious matter concerns whether the measures and their associated scaling approaches *should* meet the recommended psychometric tests. Most analysts would agree with this proposition. This does not stop disputation over the feasibility of undertaking some of the tests, a good example being the difficulties experienced in obtaining suitable tests of construct validity. But this simply means that further work is required to meet exacting methodological standards. More disputatious would be the contention that what art there is in description, evaluation and decision-making might be lost in meeting such standards. It is difficult to know how to address this contention briefly, if indeed one should try, since this would mean dealing with the basis of (scientific) knowledge and its application. Perhaps the whole psychometric approach will eventually be abandoned but such speculation will not be pursued here! Another debate concerns the best scaling measure to use. Despite attempts by many researchers to try and test the different scaling methods in a variety of settings, or even in some instances to use the alternative scaling methods as tests of validity for each other, one cannot escape the impression, in reading the relevant literature, that particular (groups of) researchers become advocates for their favoured method(s). Clearly context matters here: what constitutes the best scaling method for one purpose or in one setting, may not be appropriate in other circumstances.

Unfortunately this still leaves some awkward questions: why, for example do the different scaling methods produce different (numerical) results/values when purporting to measure the *same* phenomena such as health states or quality-of-life variables? Perhaps such difficulties are simply reflecting the problem of the lack of conceptual focus which was outlined above. 'What lack of conceptual focus?' some analysts would say: if we adopt the working hypothesis that people attempt to maximise expected utility then we can use the standard gamble method and its variants. But this is a big 'if', other analysts would claim. These contentions should give an indication of the nature of the debate. It can be judged that there *is* a form of consensus amongst analysts: much more work needs to be undertaken both theoretically and empirically in this controversial area of scaling. Observation of the extensive literature in this area suggests that this is being taken seriously.

Whose Values?

Another controversial aspect of scaling has been over who is to do the rating or valuations. The discussion of Chapter 5 will not be repeated here, but one important trend ought to brought out in this concluding commentary, and this is the strong focus on the patient and the patient's perspectives that appears to be in train, not just in the scaling context but across the whole area of health status and quality of life. What is the evidence for this assertion? First, formal measures of patient satisfaction are proving more popular. Patient satisfaction (or dissatisfaction) with the processes involved in medical treatment or other health intervention, and of course with the outcome, is being more widely assessed. Indeed one of the senior figures in quality measurement, Donabedian (1988a), has argued that patient satisfaction is a crucial element in outcome evaluation. Meanwhile another senior figure, Feinstein (in Parkerson *et al.*, 1992), has made the following plea: 'I believe that what is needed for the 21st century is another conceptual revolution that will restore the patient to the focus of attention.' Moreover several commentators at the Washington conference pointed to the potential value of health status and quality-of-life measurement for patients in informing themselves about their health (and quality of life). Such additional information could help in the 'agency relationship' between doctor and patient, especially of course if health status measurement enhanced the doctor's knowledge at the same time!

Finally, it has been argued that patients should help actually design health status and quality-of-life measures (Neuberger, 1993): this would certainly represent a considerable increase in patient 'empowerment' and might go some way to meeting the concerns of those who feel that health status measurement has become dominated by the 'expert', to the possible detriment of the citizen (Carr-Hill, 1985; Ashmore *et al.*, 1989).

Concluding Remarks

The main intention of this book has been to provide a perspective on the rapidly developing field of health status and health-related quality-of-life measurement which emphasises the process of change. Indeed the developments have been so rapid and so extensive that it is not easy to 'keep up' with the field. Katz and his colleagues could scarcely have anticipated, as they laboured over the domains of the activities of daily living some 35 years ago that they would be part of a movement which led to such ambitious activities as the calculation of health state utilities and quality-adjusted life-years!

It is manifestly apparent that we have been dealing with a multi-disciplinary set of activities. Clearly each discipline has its own (analytical) perspectives: this book has been placed within a largely economic framework. All sorts of issues have been considered and various controversies and debates reported. Formal health status measurement will not 'go away' in the near future, despite some powerful critiques that have been raised about various aspects of this measurement. We have reported on some of the critical comment. So long as resources remain scarce and choices have to be made, however, measures of outcome will be required.

Two significant notes of caution will now be entered. First, anybody reviewing the vast flow of published material will be struck by the relative lack of *independent* critiques of the measures on offer, 'relative' of course because such material does exist but compared with the lengthy list of empirical applications of the measures themselves it is rather scarce. The advent of textbooks in the area is beginning to address this problem, but much more could be accomplished.

The second worry is closely related, and this concerns the uncritical application of the measures on offer. Where this is the case it is argued that the necessity for careful and creative appraisal is ignored: particular measures might be used in totally inappropriate settings and/or in ways not envisaged by the instrument developers. The discipline of economics contains a relevant example. In the late 1960s cost-benefit analysis (CBA) was advocated as a major technique for evaluation of public sector projects, with the associated claim that the use of CBA would aid rational decision-making. There is nothing especially controversial about this claim, but the CBA approach may well have suffered from over-enthusiastic advocacy, sometimes compounded by poor empirical work and/or the application of the approach in inappropriate environments. In the health sector problems continue to this day: despite the best efforts of a number of analysts who have tried to teach the fundamentals of cost-effectiveness analysis and CBA, much of the reported empirical work fails to reach an acceptable standard (Drummond *et al.*, 1986, Udvarhelyi *et al.*, 1992.)

The rather 'mechanical' way in which health status measures can be used, in some cases involving the deployment of substantial resources for the work involved, is likely to harm the cause of those who feel that health status measurement is a useful evaluative and decision-making aid. Circumspection in the use of such devices as cost/QALY league tables would also be in order.

Despite these caveats we should not lose sight of the potential benefits of health status and quality-of-life measurement. As we have indicated, a huge amount of work is being undertaken. Some of this activity conforms to what was categorised in Chapter 1 as descriptive analysis – the attempt to measure more or less comprehensively, depending upon the context, the domains of health status and health-related quality of life. But description alone is not enough, and this approach is especially inadequate if many crucial questions of resource allocation are to be tackled. For this reason, this book has been placed explicitly within the framework of economic evaluation, with the essential requirement that resource use is married to outcome evaluation. It would be unfortunate indeed if the role of the economist in this area of endeavour were to be confined to constructing cost/QALY league tables, which can be seen from this book to be just one part of one evaluative approach, namely that of cost-utility analysis. Nevertheless many economists involved in health status measurement, including the present author, would subscribe to the evaluative approach – the search for valuations which can be used in economic appraisal. If this can be accomplished, and this book indicates we have moved at least some way along the road, then we ought to be in a position to inform policy-making, especially in the crucial area of resource allocation. Sixty-five years ago the economist Arthur Pigou (1928) stated the following in the preface to the third edition of his classic work on welfare economics: 'The complicated analyses which economists endeavour to carry through are not mere gymnastic. They are instruments for the bettering of human life.' He then urged students of 'the dismal science of Political Economy' to seek light out of the darkness by applying our knowledge to such betterment! What can sometimes seem arcane arguments over such matters as the precise properties of scaling methods, or the usefulness (or otherwise) of particular measurement instruments, or the relevance of economic analysis in the measurement of health outcomes and the quality of life, are all part of the efforts of researchers and policy analysts to shed light on what can indeed be complex matters.

When all is said and done, health status and quality-of-life measurement can only be an aid, it cannot substitute for the art of decision-taking! The health and welfare of us all is at stake, so we should try to ensure in our endeavours that we do the best we can. The changing field of measurement we have been contemplating in this book is but one aspect of these endeavours.

References

Aaronson, N.K., Bard, M., Meyerowitz, B.E. *et al.* (1991) Quality of life research in oncology: past achievements and future priorities. *Cancer*, **67** (Suppl.) 839–43.

Aaronson, N.K and Beckman, J. (eds) (1987) *The Quality of Life of Cancer Patients*. Raven Press, New York.

Ahmed, P., Coelho, G. and Kolker, A. (1979) *Toward a New Definition of Health: Psychosocial Dimension*. Plenum Press, New York.

American Psychological Association (1974) *Standards for Educational and Psychological Tests*. American Psychological Association, Washington.

Andersen, T.F. and Mooney, G. (eds) (1990) *The Challenges of Medical Practice Variations*. Macmillan, Basingstoke.

Angel, R. and Gronfein, W. (1988) The use of subjective information in statistical models. *American Sociological Review*, **53**, 464–73.

Ashmore, M., Mulkay, M. and Pinch, T. (1989) *Health and Efficiency: A Sociology of Health Economics*. Open University Press, Milton Keynes.

Avorn, J. (1984) Benefit and cost analysis in geriatric care: turning age discrimination into health policy. *The New England Journal of Medicine*. **310**, 1294–301.

Backhouse, M.E., Backhouse, R.J. and Eddy, S.A. (1992) Economic evaluation bibliography. *Health Economics*, **2** (Suppl. 1) 1–235.

Banta, H.D. (1982) *Resources for Health: Technology Assessment for Policy Making*. Praeger, New York.

Banta, H.D. and Andreasen, P.B. (1990) The political dimension in health care technology assessment programs. *International Journal of Technology in Health Care*, **6**, 115–23.

Barnum, H. (1987) Evaluating healthy days of life gained from health projects. *Social Science and Medicine*, **24**, 833–41.

Baum, F.E. and Cooke R.D. (1989) Community-health needs assessment: use of the Nottingham Health Profile in an Australian study. *The Medical Journal of Australia*, **150**, 81–90.

Bebbington, A.C. (1977) Scaling indices of disablement. *British Journal of Preventive and Social Medicine*, **31**, 122–6.

Bell, D.E., Raiffa, H. and Tversky, A. (eds) (1988) *Decision Making*. Cambridge UP, Cambridge.

Bellamy, N., Buchanan, W.W., Goldsmith, C.H., *et al.* (1988) Validation study of WOMAC: a health status instrument for measuring clinically important patient relevant outcomes to antirheumatic drug therapy in patients with osteoarthritis of the hip or knee. *Journal of Rheumatology*, **15** 1833–40.

Bergner, M. (1989). Quality of life, health status, and clinical research. *Medical Care*, **27**, S148–56.

Bergner, M., Bobbitt, R.A., Carter, W.B. and Gilson, B.S. (1981). The Sickness Impact Profile: development and final revision of a health status measure. *Medical Care*, **19**, 787–805.

Bergner, M., Bowman, M., Doyle, A. *et al.* (1992) Where do we go from here? General audience discussion. *Medical Care*, **30**, (5: Suppl.), MS231–9.

Berwick, D.M. (1988) Toward an applied technology for quality measurement in health care. *Medical Decision Making*, **8**, 253–8.

Black, D. (1989) Expensive medical and surgical technology. *International Journal of Technology Assessment in Health Care*, **5**, 308–12.

Bombardier, C. and Tugwell, P. (1982) A methodological framework to develop and select indices for clinical trials: statistical and judgemental approaches, *Journal of Rheumatology*, **9**, 753–7.

Bombardier, C. and Tugwell, P. (1987) Methodological considerations in functional assessment. *Journal of Rheumatology*, **14** (Suppl. 15) 6–10.

Bombardier, C., Tugwell, P., Sinclair, A. et al. (1982) Preference for endpoint measures in clinical trials: results of structured workshops. *Journal of Rheumatology*, **9**, 798–801.

Bombardier, C., Ware, J., Russell, I.J. et al. (1986) Auranofin therapy and quality of life in patients with rheumatoid arthritis: results of a multicenter trial. *American Journal of Medicine*, **81**, 565–78.

Bowling, A. (1991) *Measuring Health: A Review of Quality of Life Measurement Scales*. Open University Press, Milton Keynes.

Boyle, M.H. and Torrance, G.W. (1984) Developing multiattribute health indexes. *Medical Care*, **22**, 1045–57.

Bradburn N.M (1969) *The Structure of Psychological Well-Being*. Aldine, Chicago.

Brazier, J.E., Harper, R. and Jones, N.M.B. et al. (1992) Validating the SF-36 health survey questionnaire: new outcome measure for primary care. *British Medical Journal*, **305**, 160–4.

Brooks, R.G. (1991) *Health Status and Quality of Life Measurement: Issues and Developments*. The Swedish Institute for Health Economics, Lund.

Brooks, R.G., Jendteg, S., Lindgren, B. et al. (1991) EUROQOL: health-related quality of life measurement: results of the Swedish questionnaire exercise. *Health Policy*, **18**, 37–48.

Broome, J. (1988) Good, fairness and QALYs. In Bell, J.M. and Mendus, S. (eds), *Philosophy and Medical Welfare*. Suppl. to *Philosophy*. Cambridge UP, Cambridge.

Buchan, H., Gray, M., Hill, A. and Coulter, A. (1990) Preventive measures. *The Health Service Journal*, **100**, 294–5.

Buchwald, E. (1949) Functional training. *Physical Therapy Review*, **29**, 491–6.

Buckingham, K. (1993) A note on HYE (Healthy Year Equivalent). *Journal of Health Economics*, **12**, 301–9.

Bush, J.W., Anderson, J.P., Kaplan, R.M. and Blischke, W.R. (1982) Counter-intuitive preferences in health related quality of life measurement. *Medical Care*, **20**, 516–25.

Bush, J.W., Fanshel, S. and Chen, M.M. (1972) Analysis of a tuberculin testing program using a health status index. *Socio-Economic Planning Science*, **6**, 49–68.

Callahan, L.F. and Pincus, T. (1990) A clue from a self report questionnaire to distinguish RA from non-inflammatory diffuse muscoskeletal pain: The P-VAS: D-ADL ratio. *Arthritis and Rheumatism*, **33**, 1317–22.

Callahan, L.F., Brooks, R.H., Summey, J.A. and Pincus, T. (1987) Quantitative pain assessment for routine care of rheumatoid arthritis patients, using a pain scale based on an activities of daily living and a visual analog pain scale. *Arthritis and Rheumatism*, **30**, 630–6.

Carr-Hill, R.A. (1985) The evaluation of health care. *Social Science and Medicine*, **21**, 367–75.

Ceder, L. and Thorngren, K.-G. (1982) Rehabilitation after hip repair, *The Lancet*, 2:8307, 1097–8.

Chambers, L.W. (1982) Health program review in Canada: measurement of health status. *Canadian Journal of Public Health*, **73**, 26–34.
Chambers, L.W. (1983) Physical and emotional function of primary care patients: scientific requirements for the measurement of functional health status. *Journal of the American Medical Association*, **249**, 3353–5.
Chambers, L.W., MacDonald, L.A., Tugwell, P. et al. (1982) The McMaster Health Index Questionnaire as a measure of the quality of life for patients with rheumatoid arthritis. *The Journal of Rheumatology*, **9**, 780–4.
Charlton, J.R.H., Patrick, D.L. and Peach, H. (1983) Use of multivariate measures of disability in health surveys. *Journal of Epidemiology and Community Medicine*, **37**, 296–304.
Clyne, D. and Tolley, K. (1992) Discounting of health benefits in the pharmacoeconomic analysis of drug therapies: an issue for debate? *PharmacoEconomics*, **2**, 153–62.
Cochrane, A.L. (1972) *Effectiveness and Efficiency*. Nuffield Provincial Hospital Trust, London.
Convery, F.R., Minteer, M.A., Amiel, D. and Connett, K.L. (1977) Polyarticular disability: a functional assessment. *Archives of Physical Medicine and Rehabilitation*, **58**, 494–9.
Cox, R.D., Fitzpatrick, R. and Fletcher, A.E. et al. (1992) Quality-of-life assessment: can we keep it simple? *Journal of the Royal Statistical Society*, **155**, 353–93.
Criteria Committee of the New York Heart Association, Inc. (1964) *Disease of the Heart and Blood Vessels: Nomenclature and Criteria for Diagnosis*, 6th edn. Little, Brown, Boston.
Croog, S.H., Levine, S. and Testa, M.A. (1986) The effects of antihypertensive therapy on the quality of life. *The New England Journal of Medicine*, **314**, 1657–64.
Culyer, A.J. and Wagstaff, A. (1993) QALYs versus HYEs. *Journal of Health Economics*, **12**, 311–23.
Daniels, N. Is the Oregon rationing plan fair? (1991) *Journal of the American Medical Association*, **265**, 2232–8.
DCCT Research Group. (1987) Diabetes control and complications trial (DCCT): Results of a feasibility study. *Diabetes Care*, **10**, 1.
Department of Health (1989a) *Working for Patients*. HMSO, London.
Department of Health (1989b) *Medical Audit. Working Paper 6*, HMSO, London.
Department of Health and Social Security (1976) *Sharing Regimes for Health in England*. Report of The Resource Allocation Working Party. HMSO, London.
Doll, R. (1992) Sir Austin Bradford Hill and the progress of medical science. *British Medical Journal*, **305**, 1521–6.
Dominion Bureau of Statistics and Department of National Health and Welfare (1956) *Canadian Sickness Survey 1950–1951*. Queens Printer, Ottawa.
Donabedian, A. (1966) Evaluating the quality of medical care. *Milbank Memorial Fund Quarterly*, **44**, 166–203.
Donabedian, A. (1988a) Quality and cost: choices and responsibilities. *Inquiry*, **25**, 90–9.
Donabedian, A. (1988b) Quality assessment and assurance: unity of purpose, diversity of means. *Inquiry*, **25**, 173–92.
Donabedian, A. (1989) The end results of health care: Ernest Codman's contribution to quality assessment and beyond. *The Milbank Quarterly*, **67**, 233–56.
Donabedian, A., Wheeler, J.R.C. and Wyszewianski, L. (1982) Quality, cost, and health: an integrative model. *Medical Care*, **20**, 975–92.

Donabedian, A., Elinson, J., Spitzer, W. and Tarlov, A. (1987) Advances in Health Assessment conference discussion panel. *Journal of Chronic Diseases*, **40**, (Suppl. 1), 183–91.
Donaldson, C. and Wright, K. (1989) Programme specific QALYs: a reply, *Journal of Health Economics*, **8**, 489–91.
Donaldson, C., Atkinson, A. and Bond, J. (1988) Should QALYs be programme-specific? *Journal of Health Economics*, **7**, 239–57.
Drossman, D.A., Patrick, D.L., Mitchell, C.M. et al. (1989) Health-related quality of life in inflammatory bowel disease: assessment of functional status and patient worries and concerns. *Digestive Diseases and Sciences*, **34**, 1379–86.
Drummond, M.F. (1989) Output measurement for resource allocation decisions in health care. *Oxford Review of Economic Policy*, **5**, 59–74.
Drummond, M.F., Ludbrook, A., Lowson, K.V. and Steele, A. (1986) *Studies in Economic Appraisal in Health Care Vol. 2*. Oxford University Press, Oxford.
Drummond, M.F., Stoddart, G.L. and Torrance, G.W. (1987) *Methods for the Economic Evaluation of Health Care Programmes*. Oxford UP, Oxford.
Dupuy, H.J. (1984) The Psychological General Well-Being Index (PGWB) In Wenger N.K., Mattson, M.E., Fuberg, C.D. and Elinson, J. (eds) *Assessment of Quality of Life in Clinical Trials of Cardiovascular Therapies*. Le Jacq, New York.
Eddy, D. (1990a) Clinical Decision Making: Practice Policies: What Are They? *Journal of the American Medical Association*, **236**, 877–80.
Eddy, D. (1990b) Clinical Decision Making: Practice Policies: Where do they come from? *Journal of the American Medical Association*, **263**, 1265–75.
Eddy, D.M. and Billings, J. (1988) The quality of medical evidence: implications for quality of care. *Health Affairs*, **7**, 19–32.
Edlund, M. and Tancredi, L.R. (1985) Quality of life: an ideological critique. *Perspectives in Biology and Medicine*, **28**, 591–607.
Euroqol Group, The (1990) Euroqol – a new facility for the measurement of health related quality of life. *Health Policy*, **16**, 199–208.
Fairbank, J.C.T., Couper, J., Davies, J.B., and O'Brien J.P. (1980) Oswestry low-back pain disability questionnaire. *Physiotherapy*, **66**, 271–3.
Feeny, D.H. and Torrance, G.W. (1989). Incorporating utility-based quality-of-life assessment measures in clinical trials. *Medical Care*, **27** (3: Suppl.), S191–S204.
Feinstein, A.R. (1988) Scientific standards in epidemiologic studies of the menace of daily life. *Science*, **242**, 1257–63.
Feinstein, A.R., Josephy, B.R. and Wells, C.K. (1986) Scientific and clinical problems in indexes of functional disability. *Annals of Internal Medicine*, **105**, 413–20.
Fillenbaum, G.G. (1988) *Multidimensional Functional Assessment of Older Adults: the Duke Older Americans Resources and Services Procedures*. Erlbaum, New Jersey.
Fitzpatrick, R. (1993) Contrasting approaches to quality of life in health. Paper presented at the ESRC/SHHD Workshop on The Quality of Life, Edinburgh.
Flanagin, A. and Lundberg, G. (1990) Clinical decision-making. Promoting the jump from theory to practice. *Journal of the American Medical Association*, **263**, 279–80.
Fletcher, A.E. (1993) Quality of life measures in health care. Paper presented at the ESRC/SHHD Workshop on the Quality of Life, Edinburgh.
Forer, S.K. (1981) *Revised Functional Status Rating Instrument*. Rehabilitation Institute, Glendale Adventist Medical Center, Glendale, California.
Fries, J.F. (1983) Towards an understanding of patient outcome measurement. *Arthritis and Rheumatism*, **26**, 697–704.

Fries, J.F., Spitz, P., Kraines, R.G. and Holman, R. (1980) Measurement of patient outcome in arthritis. *Arthritis and Rheumatism*, **23**, 137–45.
Froberg, D.G. and Kane, R.L. (1989a) Methodology for measuring health state preferences I: Measurement strategies. *Journal of Clinical Epidemiology*, **42**, 345–54.
Froberg, D.G. and Kane, R.L. (1989b) Methodology for measuring health state preferences II: Scaling methods. *Journal of Clinical Epidemiology*, **42**, 459–71.
Froberg, D.G. and Kane, R.L. (1989c) Methodology for measuring health state preferences III: Population and context effects: *Journal of Clinical Epidemiology*, **42**, 585–92.
Froberg, D.G. and Kane, R.L. (1989d) Methodology for measuring health state preferences IV: Progress and a research agenda. *Journal of Clinical Epidemiology*, **42**, 675–85.
Fugl-Meyer, A. and Jääskö, L. (1980) Post-stroke hemiplegia and ADL-performance. *Scandinavian Journal of Rehabilitation Medicine*, Suppl. 7, 149–52.
Gafni, A. (1991) Willingness-to-pay as a measure of the benefits. Relevant questions in the context of public decision making about health care programs. *Medical Care*, **29**, 1246–52.
Gafni, A. and Birch, S. (1993) QALYs versus HYEs: An economic perspective. Paper presented at the ESRC/SHHD Workshop on the Quality of Life, Edinburgh.
Gafni, A., Birch, S., and Mehrez A. (1993) Economics, health and health economics; HYEs versus QALYs. *Journal of Health Economics*, **12**, 325–39.
Ganz, P.A. (1990) Methods of assessing the effect of drug therapy on quality of life. *Drug Safety*, **5**, 233–42.
Garrad, J. and Bennett, A.E. (1971) A validated interview schedule for use in population surveys of chronic disease and disability. *British Journal of Preventive and Social Medicine*, **25**, 97–104.
Gerrard, K. (1991) *A Review of Cost Utility Studies: Assessing Their Policy-making Relevance*. Health Economics Research Unit Discussion Paper 11, Aberdeen.
Goldberg, D. (1978) *Manual of the General Health Questionnaire*. NFER Publishing, Windsor.
Goldberg, D.P. and Williams, P. (1988) *Users Guide to the General Health Questionnaire*. NFER-Nelson, Windsor.
Goldberg, H.I., Pantell, R.H., and Weber, J.R. (1992) Finale panel: reactions reflections, and predictions. *Medical Care*, **30**, (5:Suppl.), MS283–MS293.
Goldman, L., Hashimoto, B., Cook, E.F.L. and Loscalzo, A. (1981) Comparative reproducibility and validity of systems for assessing cardiovascular functional class: advantages of a new specific activity scale. *Circulation*, **64**, 1227–34.
Granger, C.V. (1982) Health accounting – functional assessment of the long-term patient. In Kottke, F.J., Stilwell, G.K. and Lehman J.F. (eds) *Krusen's Handbook of Physical Medicine and Rehabilitation*. W.B. Saunders, Philadelphia.
Granick, S. (1983) Psychologic assessment technology for geriatric practice. *Journal of the American Geriatrics Society*, **31**, 728–42.
Greenwald, H.P. (1987) The specificity of quality-of-life measures among the seriously ill. *Medical Care*, **25**, 642–51.
Gudex, C. and Kind, P. (1988) *The QALY Toolkit*. Centre for Health Economics Discussion Paper 38, York.
Gudex, C. and Kind, P. (1993) *Scaling Methods for Health State Valuations: Rosser Revisited*. Centre for Health Economics Discussion Paper 107, York.
Gurland, B., Kuriansky, J., Sharpe, L. et al. (1977) The Comprehensive Assessment and Referral Evaluation (CARE) – rationale, development and reliability. *International Journal of Aging and Human Development*, **8**, 9–42.

Guyatt, G.H., (1988) Measuring health status in chronic airflow limitation. *European Respiratory Journal*, **1**, 560–4.
Guyatt, G.H., Bombardier, C. and Tugwell, P. (1986) Measuring disease-specific quality of life in clinical trials. *Canadian Medical Association Journal*, **134**, 889–95.
Guyatt, G.H., Berman, L.B., Townsend, M. *et al.* (1987) A measure of quality of life for clinical trials in chronic lung diseases. *Thorax*, **42**, 773–8.
Guyatt, G.H., Deyo, R.A., Charlson, M. *et al.* (1989a) Responsiveness and validity in health status measurement: a clarification. *Journal of Clinical Epidemiology*, **42**, 403–8.
Guyatt, G.H., Mitchell, A., Irvine, E.J. *et al.* (1989b) A new measure of health status for clinical trials in inflammatory bowel disease. *Gastroenterology*, **96**, 804–10.
Haber, P.A.L. (1986) Technology in aging. *The Gerontologist*, **26**, 350–7.
Hadorn, D.C. (1991) Setting health care priorities in Oregon: cost-effectiveness meets the rule of rescue. *Journal of the American Medical Association*, **265**, 2218–25.
Haes, J.C.J.M. de, Pruyn, J.F.A. and Knippenberg, F.C. van. (1983) Klachtenlijst voor kankerpatienten. Eerste ervaringen. *Nederlands Tijdschrift voor de Psychologie*, **38**, 403–22.
Haig, T.H.B., Scott, D.A. and Wickett, L.I. (1986) The rational zero point for an illness index with ratio properties. *Medical Care*, **24**, 113–24.
Haig, T.H.B., Scott, D.A. and Stevens, G.B. (1989) Measurement of the discomfort component of illness. *Medical Care*, **27**, 280–7.
Hanslukwa, H.E. (1985) Measuring the health of populations. Indicators and interpretations. *Social Science and Medicine*, **20**, 1207–24.
Harris, J. (1987) QALYfying the value of life. *Journal of Medical Ethics*, **13**, 117–23.
Harvey, R.F. and Jellinek, H.M. (1981) Functional performance assessment: a program approach. *Archives of Physical Medicine and Rehabilitation*, **62**, 456–61.
Helewa, A., Goldsmith, C.H. and Smythe, H.A. (1982) Independent measurement of functional capacity in rheumatoid arthritis. *The Journal of Rheumatology*, **9**, 794–7.
Illich, I. (1975) *Medical Nemesis*. Calder and Boyar, London.
Jette, A.M. (1980) Functional Status Index: reliability of a chronic disease evaluation instrument. *Archives of Physical Medicine and Rehabilitation*, **61**, 395–401.
Jette, A.M., Davies, A.R., Cleary, P.D. *et al.* (1986) The Functional Status Questionnaire: reliability and validity when used in primary care. *Journal of General Internal Medicine*, **1**, 143–9.
Johansen, K.S. (1989) Health care technology and quality around the world. In *Hospital Management International '89*. International Hospital Federation. Sabercrown Publishing, London.
Joyce, C.R.B. (1983) Sociopharmacology and social benefits: the relevance of judgement analysis to drug development. In Teeling Smith, G. (ed.) *Measuring the Social Benefits of Medicine*. Office of Health Economics, London.
Kane, R.L. (1990) Promoting the art of the possible in long-term care. *American Journal of Public Health*, **80**, 15–16.
Kaplan, R.M. (1982) Human preference measurement for health decisions and the evaluation of long-term care. In Kane, R.L. and Kane, R.A. (eds) *Values and Long-Term Care*. Lexington Books, Lexington.
Kaplan, R.M., Bush, J.W. and Berry, C. (1976) Health status: types of validity and the index of well-being. *Health Service Research*, **11**, 478–507.
Karnofsky, D.A. and Burchenal, J.H. (1949) The clinical evaluation of chemotherapeutic agents in cancer. In Macleod, C.M., *Evaluation of Chemotherapeutic Agents*.

Columbia UP, New York.
Kassirer, J.P., Moskowitz, A.J., Lau, J. and Pauker, S.G. (1987) Decision analysis: a progress report. *Annals of Internal Medicine*, **106**, 275–91.
Katz, S. (1983) Assessing self-maintenance: activities of daily living, mobility, and instrumental activities of daily living. *Journal of the American Geriatrics Society*, **31**, 721–7.
Katz, S. and Akpom, C.A. (1976) A measure of primary sociobiological functions. *International Journal of Health Services*, **6**, 493–508.
Katz, S., Ford, A.B., Moskowitz, R.W. *et al.* (1963) Studies of illness in the aged; the index of ADL: a standardized measure of biological and psychosocial function. *Journal of the American Medical Association*, **185**, 914–17.
Kawachi, I, (1989) QALYs and justice. *Health Policy*, **13**, 115–20.
Kind, P. and Carr-Hill, R. (1987) The Nottingham Health Profile: a useful tool for epidemiologists? *Social Science and Medicine*, **8**, 905–10.
Kind, P., Rosser R. and Williams A. (1982) Valuation of quality of life: some psychometric evidence. In Jones-Lee. M. (ed.) *The Value of Life and Safety*. North Holland, Amsterdam.
Krahn, M. and Gafni, A. (1992) *Discounting in the Economic Evaluation of Health Care Interventions: From Practice to Theory to Practice*. Working Paper Series No. 92–2, CHEPA, McMaster University, Hamilton, Ontario.
Kuriansky, J.B. and Gurland, B. (1976) Performance test of activities of daily living. *International Journal of Aging and Human Development*, **7**, 343–52.
Kurtzke, J.F. (1983) Rating neurologic impairment in multiple sclerosis: an expanded disability status scale (EDSS). *Neurology*, **33**, 1444–52.
Lancaster, H.O. (1974) *An Introduction to Medical Statistics*. John Wiley, New York.
Langner, T.S. and Michael, S.T. (1963) *Life Stress and Mental Health*. The Free Press of Glencoe, Collier-Macmillan, London.
Lawton, M.P. (1972) Assessing the Competence of Older People. In Kent D., Kastenbaum, R. and Sherwood, S., *Research Planning and Action for the Elderly*. Behavioural Publications, New York.
Lawton, M.P. and Brody, E.M. (1969) Assessment of older people: self-maintaining and instrumental activities of daily living. *The Gerontologist*, **9**, 179–86.
Lawton, M.P., Moss, M., Fulcomer, M. and Kleban, M.H. (1982) A research and service oriented multilevel assessment instrument. *Journal of Gerontology*, **37**, 91–9.
Lehmann, A.F. (1987) Joint commission sets agenda for change. *Quality Review Bulletin*, **13**, 148–50.
Levine, M.N., Guyatt, G.H., Gent, M. *et al.* (1988) Quality of life in stage II breast cancer: an instrument for clinical trials. *Journal of Clinical Oncology*, **6**, 1798–1810.
Linn, M.W. and Linn, B.S. (1982) The rapid disability rating scale. *Journal of the American Geriatrics Society*, **30**, 378–82.
Lipscomb, J. (1989). Time preferences for health in cost-effectiveness analysis. *Medical Care*, **27** (3 Suppl.) S233–53.
Logan, W.P.D. and Lambert, P.M. (1979) Vital Statistics. In Hobson, W. (ed.) *The Theory and Practice of Public Health*. Open University Press, Milton Keynes.
Lohr, K.N. (1992) Fostering the application of health state measures in clinical settings: Proceedings of a conference. *Medical Care*, **30**, (Suppl. 5), MS1–293.
Loomes, G. (1988) Disparities Between Health State Measures: An Explanation and Some Implications. Paper presented to Health Economists' Study Group Meeting, Brunel University, Uxbridge.

Loomes, G. and McKenzie, L. (1989) The use of QALYs in health care decision making. *Social Science and Medicine*, **28**, 299–308.
Loomes, G. and Sugden, R. (1987) Some implications of a more general form of regret theory. *Journal of Economic Theory*, **41**, 270–87.
McCartney, C.F. and Larson, D.B. (1987) Quality of life in patients with gynecological cancer. *Cancer*, **60** (Suppl.) 2129–36.
McClatchie, G., Schuld, W. and Goodwin, S. (1983) A maximized-ADL index of functional status for stroke patients. *Scandinavian Journal of Rehabilitation Medicine*, **15**, 155–63.
McDowell, I. and Newell, C. (1987) *Measuring Health: A Guide to Rating Scales and Questionnaires*. Oxford University Press, New York and Oxford.
McEwen, J. (1983) The Nottingham Health Profile, A measure of perceived health. In Teeling Smith, G. (ed.) *Measuring the Benefits of Medicines*. Office of Health Economics, London.
McGlynn, E.A., Norquist, G.S., Wells, K.B. et al. (1988) Quality-of-care research in mental health: responding to the challenge. *Inquiry*, **25**, 157–70.
Macmillan, A.M. (1957) The health opinion survey: technique for estimating prevalence of psychoneurotic and related types of disorders in communities. *Psychological Reports*, **3**, 325.
McNair, D.M.L., Lorr, M. and Doppleman, L.F. (1971) *Manual for the Profile of Mood States*. Educational and Industrial Service, San Diego.
McWhinnie, J.R. (1981) Disability assessment in population surveys. *Revue D'Epidémiologie et de Santé Publique*, **29**, 413–19.
Mahler, D.H., Weinberg, D.M., Wells, C.K. and Feinstein, A.R. (1984) The measurement of dypsnoea: contents, interobserver agreement, and physiologic correlates of two new clinical indexes. *Chest*, **85**, 751–8.
Mahoney, F.I. and Barthel, D.W. (1965) Functional evaluation: the Barthel index. *Maryland State Medical Journal*, **14**, 61–5.
Maynard, A. (1991) Developing the Health Care Market. *Economic Journal*, **101**, 1277–86.
Maynard, A. (1993) Future directions for health care reform. In Drummond, M.F. and Maynard, A. (eds) *Purchasing and Providing Cost-Effective Health Care*. Churchill Livingstone, Edinburgh.
Meenan, R.F., Gertman, P.M. and Mason, J.H. (1980) Measuring health status in arthritis: The Arthritis Impact Measurement Scales. *Arthritis and Rheumatism*, **23**, 146–52.
Meenan, R.F., Gertman, P.M., Mason, J.H. and Dunaif, R. (1982) The Arthritis Impact Measurement Scales. *Arthritis and Rheumatism*, **25**, 1048–53.
Meenan, R.F., Mason, J.H. and Anderson, J.J. et al. (1992) The content and properties of a revised and expanded Arthritis Impact Measurement Scales health status questionnaire. *Arthritis and Rheumatism*, **35**, 1–10.
Mehrez, A. and Gafni, A. (1991) The healthy-years equivalent: how to measure them using the standard gamble approach. *Medical Decision Making*, **11**, 140–6.
Melzack, R. (1975) The McGill Pain Questionnaire: major properties and scoring methods. *Pain*, **1**, 277–99.
Mistiaen, P. and Harteveld, J.v. (1992) A comment on the Duke University Center Health Profile. *Medical Care*, **30**, 471–2.
Miyamoto, J.M. and Eraker, S.A. (1985) Parameter estimates for a QALY utility model. *Medical Decision Making*, **5**, 191–213.
Mor, V. and Guadagnoli, E. (1988) Quality of life measurement: a psychometric tower of babel. *Journal of Clinical Epidemiology*, **41**, 1055–8.
Moskowitz, E. and McCann, G.G. (1957) Classification of disability in chronically

ill and aging. *Journal of Chronic Diseases*, **5**, 342–6.
Mosteller, F., Ware, J.E. and Levine, S. (1989) Finale panel: comments on the conference on Advances in Health Status Assessment. *Medical Care*, **27**, S282–94.
Mulley, A.G. (1989) Assessing patients' utilities: can the ends justify the means? *Medical Care*, **27**, S269–81.
Murley, R. (1989). Letter. *British Medical Journal*, **298**, 1032–3.
Nelson, E.C. and Berwick, D.M. (1989) The measurement of health status in clinical practice. *Medical Care*, **27**, S77–S90.
Nelson, E., Conger, B., Douglass, R. *et al.* (1983) Functional health status levels of primary care patients. *Journal of the American Medical Association*, **249**, 3331–8.
Nelson, E., Wasson, J., Kirk, J. *et al.* (1987) Assessment of function in routine clinical practice: description of the Coop Chart method and preliminary findings. *Journal of Chronic Diseases*, **40**, 55S–63S.
Neuberger, J. (1993) The public face of outcomes. *The Health Service Journal*, 25 February 1993:19.
Nord, E. (1992) An alternative to QALYs: the saved young life equivalent (SAVE) *British Medical Journal*, **305**, 875–7.
Nou, E. and Aberg, T (1980) Quality of survival in patients with surgically treated bronchial carcinoma. *Thorax*, **35**, 255–63.
O'Brien, W. (1989) Letter. *The Journal of Rheumatology*, **16**, 849–50.
Olsson, G., Lubsen, J., van Es. G. and Rehnquist, N. (1986) Quality of life after myocardial infarction: effect of long-term metoprolol on mortality and morbidity. *British Medical Journal*, **292**, 1491–3.
Parkerson, G.R., Gehlbach, S.H., Wagner, E.H. *et al.* (1981). The Duke-UNC health profile: an adult health status instrument for primary care. *Medical Care*, **19**, 806–23.
Parkerson, G.R., Broadhead, W.E. and Chiu-kit, J. (1990) The Duke health profile: a 17-item measure of health and dysfunction. *Medical Care*, **28**, 1057–72.
Parkerson, G.R., Deyo, R.A., Golden, W.E. *et al.* (1992) Strategies for improving and expanding the application of health status measures in clinical settings: general audience discussion. *Medical Care*, **30**, (5:Suppl.) MS210–18.
Patrick, D.L. and Deyo, R.A. (1989) Generic and disease-specific measures in assessing health status and quality of life. *Medical Care*, **27**, S217–32.
Patrick, D.L. and Peach H. (1989) *Disablement in the Community*. Oxford UP, Oxford.
Patrick, D.L., Bush, J.W. and Chen, M.M. (1973) Methods for measuring levels of well-being for a health status index. *Health Services Research*, **8**, 228–45.
Pearlman, R.A. (1987) Development of a functional assessment questionnaire for geriatric patients: the Comprehensive Older Persons' Evaluation (COPE). *Journal of Chronic Diseases*, **40**, (Suppl. 1) 85S–94S.
Pfeffer, R.I., Kurosaki, T.T., Harrah, C.H. *et al.* (1982) Measurement of functional activities in older adults in the community. *Journal of Gerontology*, **37**, 323–9.
Pfeiffer, E., Johnson, T. and Chiofolo, R. (1981) Functional assessment of elderly subjects in four service settings. *Journal of the American Geriatrics Society*, **29**, 433–7.
Pigou, A.C. (1928) *The Economics of Welfare*, 3rd edn, Macmillan, London.
Pincus, T., Summey, J.A., Soraci, S.A. Jr. *et al.* (1983) Assessment of patient satisfaction in activities of daily living using a modified Stanford Health Assessment Questionnaire. *Arthritis and Rheumatism*, **26**, 1346–53.
Pincus, T., Callahan, L.F., Brooks, R.H. *et al.* (1989) Self-report questionnaire scores in rheumatoid arthritis compared with traditional physical, radiographic, and labo-

ratory measures. *Annals of Internal Medicine*, **110**, 259–66.
Pollack, M.M., Ruttman, U.E., Getson, P.R. *et al.* (1987) Accurate prediction of the outcome of pediatric intensive care: a new quantitative method. *New England Journal of Medicine*, **316**, 134–9.
Power, E. (1992) From the Congressional Office of Technology Assessment: Evaluation of the Oregon Medicaid proposal. *Journal of the American Medical Association*, **268**, 3292.
Priestman, T.J. and Baum, M. (1976) Evaluation of quality of life in patients receiving treatment for advanced breast cancer. *The Lancet*, (i) 899–901.
Revicki, D.A. (1990) Quality of life research in the health care industry. *Journal of Research in Pharmaceutical Economics*, **2**, 41–53.
Revicki, D.A., Rothman, R. and Luce, B. (1992) Health-related quality of life assessment and the pharmaceutical industry. *PharmacoEconomics*, **1**, 394–408.
Roberts, H. (1990) *Outcome and Performance in Health Care*. Public Finance Foundation, London.
Roland, M. and Morris, R. (1983) A study of the natural history of back pain part I: development of a reliable and sensitive measure of disability in low backpain. *Spine*, **8**, 141–4.
Rose, G.A. (1965) Ischemic heart disease. Chest pain questionnaire. *Milbank Memorial Fund Quarterly*, **43**, 32–9.
Rosow, I. and Breslow, N. (1966) A Guttmann scale for the aged. *Journal of Gerontology*, **21**, 556–9.
Rosser, R.M. (1983) A history of the development of health indicators. In Teeling Smith, G. (ed.) *Measuring the Social Benefits of Medicine*. Office of Health Economics, London.
Rosser, R.M. and Kind, P. (1978) A scale of valuations of states of illness. Is there a social consensus? *International Journal of Epidemiology*, **7**, 347–58.
Rosser, R.M., Allison, R., Butler, C. *et al.* (1993) The Index of Health-Related Quality of Life (IHQL): a new tool for audit and cost per QALY analysis. In Walker, S. and Rosser, R. (eds) *Quality of Life Assessment: Key Issues in the 1990s*. Kluwer, Dordrecht.
Rubenstein, L.Z. (1987) Geriatric assessment: an overview of its import. *Clinics in Geriatric Medicine*, **3**, 1–15.
Sarno, J.E., Sarno, M.T. and Levita, E. (1973) The Functional Life Scale. *Archives of Physical Medicine and Rehabilitation*, **54**, 214–20.
Schipper H., Clinch, J., McMurray, A. and Levitt, M. (1984) Measuring the quality of life of cancer patients: the Functional Living Index – Cancer. Development and validation. *Journal of Clinical Oncology*, **2**, 472–83.
Schoening, H.A. and Iversen, I.A. (1968) Numerical scoring of self-care status: a study of the Kenny Self-Care Evaluation. *Archives of Physical Medicine and Rehabilitation*, **49**, 221–9.
Schroeder, S.A. (1987) Outcome assessment 70 Years later: are we ready? *The New England Journal of Medicine*, **316**, 160–2.
Scott, J. and Huskisson, E.C. (1976) Graphic representation of pain. *Pain*, **2**, 175–84.
Selby, P.J., Chapman, J.A.W., Etazadi-Amoli, J. *et al.* (1984) The development of a method for assessing the quality of life of cancer patients. *British Journal of Cancer*, **50**, 13–22.
Sheikh, K., Smith, D.S., Meade, T.W. *et al.* (1979) Repeatability and validity of a modified activities of daily living (ADL) index in studies of chronic disability. *International Rehabilitation Medicine*, **1**, 51–8.
Sheldon, M.P. (1935) A physical achievement record for use with crippled children. *Journal of Health Physiology*, **6**, 30–31.

Siegler, M. (1987) Decision analysis and clinical medical ethics: beginning the dialogue. *Medical Decision Making*, **7**, 124–6.
Sintonen, H. (1981) An approach to measuring and valuing health states. *Social Science and Medicine*, **15C**, 55–65.
Slater, R.J., LaRocca, N.J. and Scheinberg, L.C. (1984) Development and testing of a minimal record of disability in multiple sclerosis. *Annals of the New York Academy of Sciences*, **436**, 453–68.
Smith, J.E., Garraway, W.M., Akhtar, A.J. et al. (1977) An assessment unit for measuring the outcome of stroke rehabilitation. *British Journal of Occupational Therapy*, **40**, 51–3.
Spilker, B. (1990) *Quality of Life Assessment in Clinical Trials*. Raven Press, New York.
Spilker, B., Molinek, F.R., Johnston, K.A. et al. (1990) Quality of life bibliography and indexes. *Medical Care*, **28**, DS1–DS77.
Spitzer, W.O., Dobson, A.J., Hall, J. et al. (1981) Measuring the quality of life of cancer patients: a concise QL index for use by physicians. *Journal of Chronic Disease*, **34**, 585–97.
Steinbrocker, O., Traeger, C.H. and Battman, R.C. (1949) Therapeutic criteria in rheumatoid arthritis. *Journal of the American Medical Association*, **140**, 653–62.
Stewart, M., Tudiver, F., Bass, M.J. et al. (1992) *Tools for Primary Care Research*. Sage Publications, Newbury Park.
Stewart, T.R. and Joyce, C.R.B. (1988) Increasing the power of clinical trials through judgement analysis. *Medical Decision Making*, **8**, 33–8.
Streiner, D.L. and Norman, G.R. (1989) *Health Measurement Scales: A Practical Guide to Their Development and Use*. Oxford, Oxford UP.
Swaroop, S. (1960) *Introduction to Health Statistics*. E. and S. Livingstone, Edinburgh.
Teeling Smith, G. (1988) Economic analysis for medicines. *Pharmaceutical Medicine*, **3**, 61–7.
Thompson, M.S. (1986) Willingness to pay and accept risks to cure chronic disease. *American Journal of Public Health*, **76**, 392–6.
Torrance, G.W. (1982) Multiattribute utility theory as a method of measuring social preferences for health states in long-term care. In Kane, R.L. and Kane, R.A. (eds) *Values and Long-Term Care*. Lexington Books, Lexington.
Torrance, G.W. (1984) Health states worse than death. In Eimermen, W.v., Engelbrecht, R. and Flagle, Ch.D. (eds) Third International Conference on System Science in Health Care, Springer Verlag, Berlin.
Torrance, G.W. (1986) Measurement of health state utilities for economic appraisal: a review. *Journal of Health Economics*, **5**, 1–30.
Torrance, G.W. (1987) Utility approach to measuring health-related quality of life. *Journal of Chronic Diseases*, **40**, 593–600.
Torrance, G.W. and Feeny, D. (1989) Utilities and quality-adjusted life years. *International Journal of Technology Assessment in Health Care*, **5**, 559–75.
Torrance, G.W., Thomas, W.H. and Sackett, D.L. (1972) A utility maximization model for evaluation of health care programs. *Health Services Research*, **7**, 118–33.
Trudel, L., Fabia, J. and Bouchard, J.-P. (1984) Quality of life of 50 carotid endarterectomy survivors: a long-term follow-up study. *Archives of Physical Medicine and Rehabilitation*, **65**, 310–12.
Tugwell, P., Bombardier, C., Buchanan, W.W. et al. (1987) The MACTAR Patient preference disability questionnaire – an individualized functional priority approach for assessing improvement in physical disability in clinical trials in rheumatoid arthritis. *Journal of Rheumatology*, **14**, 446–51.

Tuteur, P.G. (1992) Strategies for improving and expanding the application of health status measures in clinical settings. *Medical Care*, **30** (5:Suppl.) MS202–4.

Udvarhelyi, I.S., Colditz, G.A., Rai, A. and Epstein, A.M. (1992) Cost-effectiveness and cost-benefit analysis in the medical literature: are the methods being used correctly? *Annals of Internal Medicine*, **116**, 238–44.

US Department of Health, Education, and Welfare (DHEW) (1978) *Working Document on Patient Care Management*. U.S. Government Printing Office, Washington, DC.

Veit, C.T. and Ware, J.E. (1982) Measuring health and health-care outcomes. In Kane, R.L. and Kane, R.A. (eds) *Values and Long Term Care*. Lexington Books, Lexington.

Verbrugge, L.M. and Balaban, D.J. (1989) Patterns of change in disability and well-being. *Medical Care*, **27**, S128–47.

von Neumann, J. and Morgenstern, O. (1944) *Theory of Games and Economic Behavior*. Princeton University Press, Princeton.

Waddell, G. and Main, C.J. (1984) Assessment of severity in low-back disorders. *Spine*, **9**, 204–8.

Ware, J.E. and Sherbourne, C.D. (1992) The MOS 36-item short form health survey (SF-36): conceptual framework and item selection. *Medical Care*, **30**, 473–81.

Ware, J.E., Brook, R.H., Davies-Avery, A. and Lohr, K.N. (1981) Choosing measures of health status for individuals in general populations. *American Journal of Public Health*, **71**, 620–5.

Ware, J.E., Manning, W.G., Duan, N. et al. (1984) Health status and the use of outpatient mental health services. *American Psychologist*, **39**, 1090–1100.

Weinstein, M.C. (1988) A QALY is a QALY is a QALY – or is it? *Journal of Health Economics*, **7**, 289–90.

Weinstein, M.C. and Stason, W.B. (1977) Foundations of cost-effectiveness analysis for health and medical practice. *The New England Journal of Medicine*, **296**, 716–21.

Weissert, W., Wan, T.H. and Livieratos, B.B. (1979) *Effects and Costs of Day Care and Home-Maker Services for the Chronically Ill: A Randomized Experiment*. NCHSR/DHEW Report, Washington.

Wennberg, J.E., Bunker, J.P. and Barnes, B. (1980) The need for assessing the outcome of common medical practice. *Annual Reviews of Public Health*, 277–95.

Whiting, S. and Lincoln, N. (1980) An ADL assessment for stroke patients. *British Journal of Occupational Therapy*, **2**, 44–6.

Wilensky, G.R. (1991) From the Health Care Financing Administration: nursing home reform. *Journal of the American Medical Association*, **265**, 444.

Wilkin, D., Hallam, L. and Doggett, M.A. (1992) *Measures of Need and Outcome for Primary Health Care*. Oxford UP, Oxford.

Williams, A. (1985) Economics of coronary artery bypass grafting. *British Medical Journal*, **291**, 326–9.

Williams, A. (1988) Ethics and efficiency in the provision of health care. In Bell, J.M. and Mendus, S. (eds) *Philosophy and Medical Welfare*. (Suppl. to *Philosophy*, 1988) Cambridge UP, Cambridge.

Williams, A. (1993) The Euroqol instrument. Paper presented to the Health Economists' Study Group meeting, University of Strathclyde, Glasgow, July 1993.

Williamson, J.W. (1988) Future policy directions for quality assurance: lessons from the health accounting experience. *Inquiry*, **25**, 67–77.

Wolfson, A.D., Sinclair, A.J., Bombardier, C. and McGeer, A. Preference measurements for functional status in stroke patients: interrater and intertechnique comparisons. In Kane, R.L. and Kane, R.A. (eds) *Values and Long Term Care*. Lexington Books, Lexington.

Index

Aaronson, N.K. 107
Accuracy 46
Activities of Daily Living (ADL) 18, 19, 21, 22, 23, 35, 41, 63, 118, 104
Affect Balance Scale 41, 42, 104
Aggregate measures 17, 21–32, 33, 43
Ahmed, P. 7
American Journal of Public Health 63
American Psychological Association 48
American Rheumatological Association 104
Andersen, T.F. 12
Anxiety 39, 42
Arthritis 37, 85
  Arthritis Impact Measurement Scale 37–40, 104, 107
  AIMS 2 37, 38
Arthroscopy 10
Audit, medical 64–6
Auranofin trial 110

Back pain 37
Balaban, D.J. 118
Banta, H.D. 66, 91
Barthel Index 19, 20
Bergner, M. 69
Berwick, D.M. 69–70, 91–3
Bias (systematic error) 46
Billings, J. 12
Birch, S. 83
Black, D. 101
Bombardier, C. 49–52, 54, 62
British Medical Journal 65
Brazier, J. 47–48
Burden, respondent 54
  medical staff 55
Bush, J.W., Quality of Well Being (QWB) 21, 25–9, 33, 110, 114, 118
  well-year 25, 33, 82

Cancer 9–10, 37, 52

Captopril 110
Cardinal measurement 72–73
Cardiovascular disease 103
Category rating 73
Category scaling 73–75
Chambers, L.W. 46
Chronic lung disease 37
Classification: health status measures 17
  illness states: Rosser 31
Clinical
  decision-making 93, 98–9
  ethics 96–8
  judgement analysis 86
  practice 106–9
  reality 93
  sensibility 54, 68
  trials 109–11
Cochrane, A.L. 94–6
Codman, A. 60, 102
Comprehensiveness 50
Concurrent validity 51
Condition-specific measures 17
Construct validity 50, 51–2
Content validity 49–50
Convergent validity 51–2
COOP charts 34, 106, 107
Cost analysis 2, 3
Cost–benefit analysis 2, 3, 5–6, 81, 122
Cost-effectiveness analysis 2, 3, 4, 81, 109, 114, 123
Cost measurement 2–3
Cost-minimisation analysis 2, 3, 4
Costing of randomised control trials 96
Cost per QALY 82, 83, 123
  league tables 111, 113–14, 123
Cost-utility analysis 2, 3, 4–5, 6, 81, 83, 109, 123
Credibility 49, 50
Criterion validity 50, 51
Cox, R.D. 92
Cronbach's α test 47
Croog, S.H. 110

Index

Data: hard/soft distinction 40, 62–3
Decision analysis 78
Decision-making: clinical 98–9, 106–9
  and health services research 91–3
Demographic change 11
Depression 39, 42
Descriptors: health state 16, 24, 35
Determination of social weights 16, 24
Dexterity 39
Diabetes 37, 40
Diagnosis 61
Dickens, C. 9
Digestive diseases 37
Disability 17, 18, 30–1, 50, 51
Diseases of medical progress (DOMPS) 11
Disease-specific measures 17, 87
Distress–disability matrix 33
Dominion Bureau of Statistics, Canada 17
Donabedian, A. 58–60, 64
Drummond, M. 83
DUKE Profile 52
Duke University Centre Health Profile (DUHP) 34, 35, 55
Dynamics 117–19

Economic evaluation 2–7, 123
  and drugs 110, 111
  and QALYs 111
Eddy, D. 12, 98–9
Edlund, M. 67–8
Effectiveness, medical 6, 14, 57, 101
Efficiency 6, 14, 57
End-result method 60
Equity 6, 57, 83, 84
Equivalence 80
Eraker, S.A. 43
Ethics and clinical trials 94–5
Ethics, medical and health status measurement 96–8
Euroqol 32, 33, 75, 87, 88
Evaluation: economic 2–3
Expected life years 82
Expected utility 77
Explicit measurement methods 70
Externalities 97

Face validity 49, 50
Farr, W. 16, 102

Feasibility 50
Feinstein, A.R. 18, 53, 94, 120
Financial incentives 108–9
Flanagin, A. 93
Fletcher, A.E. 105
Fries, J.F. 40, 60
Froberg, D.G. 80–1
Functional assessment measures 17–21, 35, 93
Functional Limitations Profile (FLP) 33
Function-specific measures 17
Functional Status Index (FSI) 20, 21, 104
Functional Status Questionnaire (FSQ) 21, 22–3, 107

Gafni, A. 83
Ganz, P.A. 110
Generic measures 17, 18, 24, 32, 33, 41, 43, 84, 105
General Health Questionnaire 41, 42, 106, 107
General health status measures 17, 21
General Well-being Schedule 41, 42
Generalisability 53
Geriatrics 103
Gerrard, K. 104
Global health measures 17
Goldberg, H.I. 108
Gold standard 51–2
Greenwald, H.P. 52
Granick, S. 40
Graunt, J. 16, 102
Guyatt, G.H. 35–6, 42, 53

Haber, P.A.L. 10
Hadorn, D.C. 12, 114
Haig, T.H.B. 76
Handicap 18
Hard/soft data 61–2, 68, 95
Health accounting 60
Health Assessment Questionnaire (HAQ) 37, 40, 104
Health care costs 11, 13
Health care quality measurement 92
Health Care Financing Administration 63
Health: definition of 7–8
Health Maintenance Organisations 13
Health measurement: empirical approach 117
  theoretical approach 117

Health-related quality of life 7, 15, 69, 102, 116, 123
Health services research and decision-making 91–3
Health status descriptors 16
Health status indicators 15
Health status indexes 15, 69
Health status measurement 16, 54, 86, 108, 122, 123
  applications in clinical practice 106–9
  applications in pharmaceuticals 109–11
  barriers to clinical use of 107
  methodological criteria 46
  rising interest in 8–14
  scaling methods 73–81
  steps in development 15
  theoretical foundations 116–17
Health status surveys 15
Health status weights 84
Health transitions 117
Health valuation; conceptual scheme 116
Healthy year equivalent (HYE) 83, 84
Heart disease measures 37
Hypertension 40, 110

Iatrogenic disease 11
Illich, I. 11
Illness status measurement 76
Implicit measurement methods 70
Impairment 18
Index of Activities of Daily Living 19, 20
Indicators of comparative mortality rates 65
Individualistic interpretation of quality 67, 92
Inputs 2
Independent audit 65
Intermediate ADL 22, 23
Internal consistency 47
Inter-observer error 47
Inter-observer variation 63
Interval scale 71–5
Instrumental activities of daily living 18, 19, 21
Interpersonal comparisons 16
Interview Schedule for Social Interaction 43

Intra-observer error 47
Item selection 15, 24, 35, 36

Johansen, K.S. 66
Joint Commission for Accreditation of Health Care Organizations 60, 92
Journal of the American Medical Association 93
Joyce, C.R.B. 62, 86
Judgement analysis 86

Kane, R.L. 63, 80, 81
Karnofsky Performance Status Scale 104
Katz Activities of Daily Living (ADL) 20, 106
Katz, S. 17, 18, 122
Keitel assessment measure 111
Kelvin temperature scale 72
Kenny functional assessment measure 19, 20
Kind, P. 30–2

Larson, D.B. 9
LASA Scale 104
Laws of Hammurabi 16
Lawton, M.P. 18
Learmonth, J. 65
Levine, M.N. 10, 13
Life expectancy 9, 82
Life Satisfaction Index 104
Life years saved 82
Logan, W.P.D. 16
London Bills of Mortality 16

Magnitude estimation 30, 75–6
Maynard, A. 113
McCartney, C.F. 9
McDowell, I. 19, 41, 43, 56, 117
McGill Pain Questionnaire 52, 104
McGlynn, E.A. 58–9
McMaster Health Index Questionnaire 34, 104
Measurement
  cardinal 72
  interval 71–5
  nominal 71, 105
  ordinal 72
  ratio 72–3, 76
Medicaid 15
Medical audit 64–66

Medical Audit News 65
Medical decisions 96–7
Medical ethics 96–8
Medical effectiveness 11–12
Meenan, R. 38–40
Mental functioning 21, 41
Mental health 103
Mental Health Inventory (MHI) 41, 42, 106
Mental health services: quality 58–9
Mental health status 40–2
Methodological criteria 17, 45–6
Methodological requirements 42
Minnesota Multiple Personality Inventory 104
Mistiaen, P. 55
Miyamoto, J.M. 43
Methyldopa 110
Mobility 19, 21, 24, 25–8
Modified HAQ 40, 63
Mooney, G. 12
Morbidity 8, 9, 110
Mortality 8, 9, 65
Multi-attribute measures 17
Multi-dimensional measures 17
Multiple sclerosis 38

Nature of measurement 15
Nelson, E. 106–8
Nervous system diseases 45
Newell, C. 19, 41, 43, 56, 117
New England Journal of Medicine 81
New York Heart Association 104
Nightingale, F. 16, 65, 71, 95, 102
Nominal measurement 105
Non-response 47
Norman, G.R. 45, 46–47
Nottingham Health Profile 34, 35, 104, 106
Nord, E. 84
Nutting, P. 108

OARS–MFAQ profile 34
O'Brien, W. 45
Oncology 103, 104, 107
Opportunity cost 2
Ordinal measurement 72
Oregon proposal 13, 114–15
Organisational and financial change 12–13
Outcome measurement 2, 58–9, 65, 68

Outcome and process controversy 61–4, 92

Pain 39, 40
Pain measurements 38, 43
Patient preferences 84, 96–8
Patient satisfaction 43, 64, 120
Patient Utility Measurement Set 110
Patrick, D.L. 76
Petty, W. 102
Pharmaceuticals and health status measurement 109–11
Pharmacoeconomics 110
Philosophy 5, 15, 85
Physical activity 25–8, 39
Physical functioning 17, 21, 22, 23
Pigou, A. 123
Population-specific measures 17
Practicality 24, 54–5
Practice policies 98–9
Prevention 2, 100–1
Priority ratings 114
Probability and standard gamble 77–8
Process 58, 59
Process measurement 62
Process measures 68
Process: outcome controversy 61–4
Productivity 83
Profiles, health 32–35
Profiles of Mood States (POMS) 52, 104
Prognosis 118
Promotion of health 2, 100–1
Propanolol 110
Psychological Adjustment to Illness Scale 104
Psychological function 22, 23
Psychological well-being 41
Psychology 15
Psychometric approaches 45
Psychometrics and scaling 119–20
PULSES profile 20, 106

Qualitative and quantitative approaches 61, 97, 112
Quality Adjusted Life Year (QALY) 3, 5, 43, 81–4, 89, 104, 111–15, 123
Quality
  adjustment 4, 86, 112
  assessment as research 69–70
  assurance 60, 66, 91

Index

framework 58–60
measurement 91
of care 58, 61, 63, 64
of life 1, 6, 7, 10, 11, 43, 57, 63, 65, 67–9, 81, 110, 111, 116
Quality of Well-Being scale 21, 24, 33, 38, 110, 114

Rand measures 34, 38, 104
Random error 46
Randomised control trials 11, 93–6, 110
Rankine temperature scale 72
Rank ordering 72
Ratio scale 72–3, 76
Rating 84–5
Rating scale 73
Rationing 12–13
Receiver operating characteristic curves 53
Resource Allocation Working Party (RAWP) 6
Regret theory 78
Rehabilitation 11, 18, 117
Relative efficiency statistic 53
Reliability 19, 24, 45, 46–8, 81, 119
Reproducibility 24, 36, 47
Resource allocation 2, 111–15
Responsiveness 36, 53, 56, 119
Revicki, D. 109, 111
Rheumatology 103, 104
Rheumatology standards 62
Rosser, R. 16
Rosser–Kind measure 30–2, 33, 43

Saved Young Life Equivalent (SAVE) 84
Scaling 15, 19, 32, 43, 71, 81, 88, 119
Scaling: category 73–5
Scores: aggregate generic measures 33
Sensibility 53
Sensitivity 50, 52
Sentinel measurement methods 70
SF-36 health profile 34
Sheldon, M.P. 18
Sickness Impact Profile 32–5, 52, 104
Siegler, M. 96–8
Simplicity in measurement 107, 108
Single score measure 24

Social
activity 22, 23, 25–8, 40
evaluation 2–3, 16, 85
functioning 13, 18, 22, 23, 24
indicators 105
health measures 43
preferences/values/weights 24, 30, 85, 87, 105
quality of life 67, 85
role 39
utility 7, 68
welfare 7
Social Maladjustment Schedule 43
Social Relationship Scale 43
Specific measures 35–40
Specificity 52
Spilker, B. 8, 45, 103
Spitzer Quality of Life Index 37, 104, 106
Standard error of measurement 48
Standard gamble scaling technique 43, 76–8, 79, 110
Stewart, T.R. 62
Streiner, D.L. 45, 46–47
Subjective
assessment 97
causal hypotheses 116
health preferences 116
judgement 56
well-being 41
soft data 62
Surgery 103, 177
Swaroop, S. 9
Swedish Institute for Health Economics 87
Symptom–problem complex 21, 24–30

Systematic error 46
Technological change 10–11
Technology assessment 66
Teeling Smith, G. 95
Tennessee Self-Concept Scale 52
Test–retest reliability 47
Theoretical foundations of health status measurement 116
Time preference and discounting 118
Time trade-off scaling method 79–80, 118
Torrance, G.W. 33, 43, 77, 82
Treatment planning 108
Tuteur, P.G. 108

Utility 5, 6, 76–7
Utility-based QALYS 43
Utility measures 15, 17, 42–3
Utility, social 58

Validity 19, 24, 48 54, 56, 81, 119
Valuation 7, 30
Values, 'whose' 84–7, 98, 120–1
Verbrugge, L.M. 118
Visual analogue scale 73

Ware, J.E. 42, 48, 117

Welfare economics 81, 83, 123
Well-being, level of 25–8
Well-year 21, 24, 33
Weinstein, M.C. 112
Wennberg, J.E. 12
Willingness to pay 6, 80–1, 110
Williamson, J.W. 60
Wilkin, D. 35, 41, 53, 56, 107
Wolfson aggregate health measure 33
World Health Organisation, definition 7, 15

Zung Self-Rating Depression Scale 52